GoodFood

101 MORE ONE-POT DISHES

D0717103

10 9 8 7 6 5 4 3 2

Published in 2009 by BBC Books,
an imprint of Ebury Publishing
A Random House Group company

Recipes © BBC Magazines 2009
Book design © Woodland Books 2009
All photographs © BBC Magazines 2009
All recipes contained within this book first
appeared in BBC *Good Food* magazine

The Random House Group Limited
Reg. No. 954009

Addresses for companies within the
Random House Group can be found at
www.randomhouse.co.uk

A CIP catalogue record for this book is available
from the British Library.

The Random House Group Limited supports
The Forest Stewardship Council (FSC), the
leading international forest certification organization.
All our titles that are printed on Greenpeace
approved FSC certified paper carry the FSC logo.
Our paper procurement policy can be found at
www.rbooks.co.uk/environment

To buy books by your favourite authors and
register for offers visit www.rbooks.co.uk

Printed and bound by Firmengruppe APPL,
aprinta druck, Wemding, Germany
Colour origination by Dot Gradations Ltd, UK

Commissioning Editor: Muna Reyal
Project Editor: Joe Cottington
Designer: Annette Peppis
Production: David Brimble
Picture Researcher: Gabby Harrington

ISBN: 9781846077678

GoodFood
101 MORE ONE-POT DISHES
TRIPLE-TESTED RECIPES

Editor
Jane Hornby

Contents

Introduction   6

Introduction

Good Food magazine's one-pot recipes are so well loved that we couldn't wait to bring you another 101 inspiring ideas. No matter what kind of cook you are, there's always an occasion when a one-pot fits the bill perfectly.

Few of us want to take on complicated cooking on a weeknight (not to mention the washing up), so quick one-pots make perfect sense when you're busy. From tasty stir-fries to soups, pasta or quick roasts, you'll find lots here that you will enjoy and that will work first time – our recipes are all triple tested to make sure of that.

One-pots are the smart way to feed a crowd, too – what could be simpler than a meal that can be prepped in advance and left virtually to cook itself while you

catch up with friends. Many of the recipes in this book, like the *Chinese-style braised beef* opposite (see p184), taste even better made a day ahead – making entertaining seriously easy.

It's not just about stews, though: one-pot cooking is for every season; for lunch, dinner or dessert. In fact, if a recipe uses just one roasting tin, wok or griddle, it's a one-pot! So bring the dish to the table, let everyone dig in, and find out just how simple good cooking can be.

Jane Hornby
Good Food magazine

Notes and conversion tables

NOTES ON THE RECIPES
• Eggs are large in the UK and Australia and extra large in America unless stated otherwise.
• Wash fresh produce before preparation.
• Recipes contain nutritional analyses for 'sugar', which means the total sugar content including all natural sugars in the ingredients, unless otherwise stated.

OVEN TEMPERATURES

Gas	°C	°C Fan	°F	Oven temp.
¼	110	90	225	Very cool
½	120	100	250	Very cool
1	140	120	275	Cool or slow
2	150	130	300	Cool or slow
3	160	140	325	Warm
4	180	160	350	Moderate
5	190	170	375	Moderately hot
6	200	180	400	Fairly hot
7	220	200	425	Hot
8	230	210	450	Very hot
9	240	220	475	Very hot

APPROXIMATE WEIGHT CONVERSIONS
• All the recipes in this book list both imperial and metric measurements. Conversions are approximate and have been rounded up or down. Follow one set of measurements only; do not mix the two.
• Cup measurements, which are used by cooks in Australia and America, have not been listed here as they vary from ingredient to ingredient. Kitchen scales should be used to measure dry/solid ingredients.

Good Food are concerned about sustainable sourcing and animal welfare so where possible, we use organic ingredients, humanely-reared meats, free-range chickens and eggs and unrefined sugar.

SPOON MEASURES

Spoon measurements are level unless otherwise specified.

- 1 teaspoon (tsp) = 5ml
- 1 tablespoon (tbsp) = 15ml
- 1 Australian tablespoon = 20ml (cooks in Australia should measure 3 teaspoons where 1 tablespoon is specified in a recipe)

APPROXIMATE LIQUID CONVERSIONS

metric	imperial	AUS	US
50ml	2fl oz	¼ cup	¼ cup
125ml	4fl oz	½ cup	½ cup
175ml	6fl oz	¾ cup	¾ cup
225ml	8fl oz	1 cup	1 cup
300ml	10fl oz/½ pint	½ pint	1¼ cups
450ml	16fl oz	2 cups	2 cups/1 pint
600ml	20fl oz/1 pint	1 pint	2½ cups
1 litre	35fl oz/1¾ pints	1¾ pints	1 quart

All this quick-and-easy chicken dish needs is a big hunk of crusty bread on the side. It's versatile too; try it stirred through pasta or as a topping for a baked potato.

Spicy tomato chicken

2 tbsp seasoned plain flour
1 tsp chilli powder
8 boneless chicken thighs
1 tbsp vegetable oil
1 onion, chopped
600ml/1 pint chicken stock
2 garlic cloves, chopped
2 tbsp tomato purée
2 courgettes, cut into chunks
450g/1lb tomatoes, quartered
small handful of fresh basil leaves, to serve

Takes 30 minutes • Serves 4

1 Mix together the seasoned flour and chilli powder. Add the chicken and toss to coat. Set aside the seasoned flour. Heat the oil in a large frying pan with a lid, add the chicken and fry for 8 minutes, until well browned, turning once. Transfer to a plate.
2 Add the onion to the pan and fry for around 5 minutes. Sprinkle over the reserved seasoned flour and cook for 1 minute, stirring all the time. Stir in the stock, garlic and tomato purée. Return the chicken to the pan and bring to the boil. Add the courgettes and tomatoes, cover and simmer for 15 minutes. Scatter with fresh basil leaves and serve.

• Per serving 424 kcalories, protein 33g, carbohydrate 19g, fat 25g, saturated fat 7g, fibre 3g, added sugar none, salt 1.2g

Do something different with your pasta and pesto – broccoli goes fantastically well with both and makes a pack of pasta go further. Eaten cold, it's a great lunchbox filler, too.

Tortellini with pesto and broccoli

140g/5oz Tenderstem or regular broccoli, cut into short lengths
250g pack fresh tortellini (ham and cheese works well)
3 tbsp fresh pesto
2 tbsp toasted pine nuts
1 tbsp balsamic vinegar
8 cherry tomatoes, halved

Takes 10 minutes • Serves 2 (easily doubled)

1 Bring a large pan of water to the boil. Add the broccoli, cook for 2 minutes, then add the tortellini and cook for 2 minutes, or according to the packet instructions.
2 Drain everything, gently rinse under cold water until cool, then tip into a bowl. Toss with the pesto, pine nuts and balsamic vinegar. Add the tomatoes. Serve warm or at room temperature.

• Per serving 573 kcalories, protein 24g, carbohydrate 64g, fat 26g, saturated fat 9g, fibre 5g, sugar 8g, salt 1.58g

Like many stews, the flavour of this meal in a bowl will actually improve if you make it ahead then re-heat it.

Speedy meatball stew

2 medium potatoes, peeled and cut into bite-sized cubes
1 tbsp olive oil
250g pack small lean beef meatballs
1 onion, chopped
2 garlic cloves, chopped
1 tbsp chopped fresh rosemary
560ml jar passata
200g/8oz frozen peas
a few Parmesan shavings, to garnish (optional)
good crusty bread, to serve

Takes 20 minutes • Serves 4

1 Boil the potatoes for 10 minutes until they are tender.
2 Meanwhile, heat the oil in a large pan. Season the meatballs, then brown them all over for about 5 minutes. Remove from the pan, drain off any excess fat, then add the onion, garlic and rosemary. Fry gently for 5 minutes.
3 Add the passata to the pan, bring to a simmer, then add the meatballs. Simmer for 5 minutes or until everything is cooked through. Add the potatoes and peas, then simmer for 1 minute. Top with the Parmesan, if using, and eat with good crusty bread.

• Per serving 286 kcalories, protein 20g, carbohydrate 28g, fat 11g, saturated fat 4g, fibre 4g, sugar 9g, salt 1.68g

Bake a basic batter mixture with a few added ingredients for a simple family supper from the storecupboard.

Cheese, bacon and onion puff

140g/5oz plain flour
4 large eggs
200ml/7fl oz milk
butter, for greasing
2 tbsp finely grated Parmesan
8 rashers ready-cooked streaky
bacon or 3 slices ham, chopped
4 spring onions, thinly sliced
140g/5oz Cheddar, grated

Takes 50 minutes • Serves 4

1 Preheat the oven to 230°C/210°C fan/ gas 8. To make the batter, tip the flour into a bowl and beat in the eggs until smooth. Gradually add the milk and carry on beating until the mix is completely lump free. Grease a large, round ceramic dish, about 22cm wide, and dust it with the grated Parmesan.
2 Tip the bacon or ham, onions and Cheddar into the batter, and stir until completely combined. Tip the batter into the prepared dish so it comes almost to the top, then bake for 30–35 minutes until puffed up and golden. Bring it to the table and serve piping hot, straight from the dish.

• Per serving 680 kcalories, protein 27g, carbohydrate 30g, fat 51g, saturated fat 18g, fibre 1g, sugar 3g, salt 2.15g

This rustic soup is super quick and cheap to make, but full of flavour.
Leave it chunky or whiz it until silky smooth – the choice is yours.

Sweet potato and rosemary soup

2 tsp olive oil, plus extra for brushing
1 onion, chopped
2 garlic cloves, crushed
750g/1lb 10oz sweet potatoes, peeled and cubed
1 litre/1¾ pints vegetable or chicken stock, plus extra (if needed)
1 fresh rosemary sprig, plus extra to garnish
toasted bread, to serve

Takes 30 minutes • Serves 4

1 Heat the oil in a large pan, then fry the onion for 5 minutes until soft. Add the garlic, then fry for 1 minute more. Stir in the sweet potatoes, then cover with the stock and bring to the boil. Strip the leaves from the rosemary sprig, and add them to the pan. Simmer for 10 minutes until the potato is soft.
2 Use a hand blender to purée the soup, adding a splash more hot water or stock if it seems too thick. Season well, then pour into warmed bowls and serve with toasted bread and a few leaves of rosemary, if you like.

• Per serving 253 kcalories, protein 13g, carbohydrate 45g, fat 4g, saturated fat 0.4g, fibre 6g, sugar 13g, salt 1.46g

Low in fat, high in iron and vitamin C, and including three of your 5-a-day, this is just about the perfect healthy stir-fry.

Sticky green stir-fry with beef

1 tbsp sunflower oil
2 × 200g/8oz sirloin steaks, trimmed of fat and thinly sliced
1 broccoli head, cut into small florets
2 garlic cloves, sliced
300g/10oz sugar snap peas
4 spring onions, thickly sliced
3 pak choi, leaves separated and cut into quarters
4 tbsp hoisin sauce

Takes 20 minutes • Serves 4

1 Heat the oil in a large wok or deep frying pan, then sizzle the beef strips for 3–4 minutes until browned. Remove and set aside. Toss the broccoli and garlic into the wok with a splash of water, then fry over a high heat for 4–5 minutes until starting to soften.

2 Add the peas, spring onions and pak choi, then stir-fry for another 2–3 minutes, then stir in the hoisin sauce and beef. Heat through quickly, adding a splash of water if it seems a little dry. Great with noodles or rice.

• Per serving 245 kcalories, protein 31g, carbohydrate 12g, fat 9g, saturated fat 2g, fibre 4g, sugar 10g, salt 0.8g

This colourful and filling salad makes a satisfying supper. Perfect for packed lunches too as it transports really well.

Beetroot, spinach and goat's cheese couscous

zest and juice of 1 large orange
140g/5oz couscous
25g/1oz walnut pieces
85g/3oz firm goat's cheese, crumbled
6 dried apricots, roughly chopped
4 small cooked beetroot, quartered
2 tbsp extra-virgin olive oil
juice of ½ lemon
2 handfuls of spinach leaves

Takes 10 minutes • Serves 2
(easily doubled)

1 Put the orange zest, juice and around 100ml/3½fl oz water in a medium pan and bring to the boil. Turn off the heat, tip in the couscous, mix well, then cover and leave to absorb for 5 minutes.

2 Fluff up the grains with a fork, then add the walnuts, cheese, apricots, beetroot and some seasoning. Mix in the oil and lemon juice (or use your favourite bought vinaigrette). If you're eating straight away, toss in the spinach now; if not, pack into a container with the spinach sat on top. When ready to eat, toss the spinach through.

• Per serving 601 kcalories, protein 21g, carbohydrate 57g, fat 34g, saturated fat 11g, fibre 5g, sugar 22g, salt 1.13g

So simple you'll make this again and again. The tomatoes and the creamy filling not only taste great but also keep the chicken dry as it cooks.

Italian stuffed chicken

2 tbsp chopped olives or sundried tomatoes
1 garlic clove, crushed
½ tsp dried mixed herbs
200g tub full-fat soft cheese (use a garlicky one, if you like)
4 plump skinless chicken breasts
4 ripe tomatoes, sliced
olive oil, for drizzling
green salad and crusty bread, to serve

Takes 25 minutes • Serves 4

1 Preheat the oven to 220°C/200°C fan/ gas 7. Beat the olives or sundried tomatoes, garlic and almost all the herbs into the cheese, then season. Cut a slit along the side of each chicken breast, then use your knife to open it out into a pocket.
2 Stuff each breast with a quarter of the cheese mix, then press to close. Lift on to a greased baking sheet. Season the top of the chicken, then overlap tomato slices over the top of each piece of chicken. Season, then scatter with the remaining herbs. Drizzle with olive oil.
3 Roast for 20 minutes until the chicken is golden around the edges and the tomatoes look a little shrivelled. Serve with a green salad and crusty bread to mop up the juices.

• Per serving 332 kcalories, protein 37g, carbohydrate 5g, fat 18g, saturated fat 9g, fibre 1g, sugar 4g, salt 1.17g

Make the most of what's in your storecupboard and freezer with this easy throw-together rice dish.

Bean and dill pilaf with garlicky yogurt

2 onions, halved and thinly sliced
25g/1oz butter
175g/6oz basmati rice
20g pack fresh dill, stalks and fronds chopped but kept separate
450ml/16fl oz vegetable stock mixed with a good pinch of saffron strands or ground turmeric
300g/10oz frozen mixed broad beans, peas and green beans
100g/4oz Greek yogurt
1 tbsp milk
1 small garlic clove, crushed

Takes 25 minutes • Serves 2 (easily doubled)

1 Fry the onions in the butter for 5 minutes until golden. Add the rice and dill stalks then stir them around the pan.
2 Pour in the saffron or turmeric stock, bring to the boil, then cover and simmer for 5 minutes. Add the beans and half the dill fronds. Cook for 5 minutes more until the liquid has been absorbed into the rice.
3 Meanwhile, stir the yogurt, milk and garlic together with some seasoning. Spoon the yogurt on top of the rice, then sprinkle with the remaining dill.

• Per serving 609 kcalories, protein 20g, carbohydrate 99g, fat 18g, saturated fat 10g, fibre 10g, sugar 13g, salt 0.63g

If your family goes mad for sausages, put this in the middle of the table and watch them dive in. The beans make a healthy and convenient change to potatoes.

Beans and bangers

1 tbsp olive oil
8 good-quality pork sausages (Toulouse or Sicilian varieties work well)
2 carrots, halved then sliced
2 onions, finely chopped
2 tbsp red wine vinegar
2 × 410g cans mixed beans in water, drained and rinsed
400ml/14fl oz chicken stock
100g/4oz frozen peas
2 tbsp Dijon mustard

Takes 40 minutes • Serves 4

1 Heat the oil in a large pan. Sizzle the sausages for about 6 minutes, turning occasionally, until brown on all sides. Remove to a plate. Tip the carrots and onions into the pan and cook for 8 minutes, stirring occasionally, until the onions are soft. Add the vinegar to the pan, then stir in the drained beans. Pour over the stock, nestle the sausages in with the beans, then simmer everything for 10 minutes.
2 Scatter in the frozen peas, cook for 2 minutes more until heated through, then take off the heat and stir in the mustard. Season to taste. Serve scooped straight from the pan.

• Per serving 569 kcalories, protein 35g, carbohydrate 41g, fat 31g, saturated fat 9g, fibre 11g, sugar 13g, salt 2.81g

It's easy to make your own version of this classic Thai street food. Better still, this version is low in fat. Use raw prawns if you can as they'll add masses more flavour than ready-cooked ones.

10-minute pad Thai

200g/8oz raw peeled prawns
1 small pack of fresh coriander, stalks finely chopped, leaves roughly chopped
2 × 200g packs straight-to-wok pad Thai noodles
85g/3oz beansprouts
1 egg, beaten
juice of 1 lime, plus wedges to serve
1 tbsp fish sauce
2 tsp sugar
1 tbsp roasted peanuts, roughly chopped, to serve

Takes 10 minutes • Serves 2 (easily doubled)

1 Dry-fry the prawns and coriander stalks in a non-stick frying pan for 1–2 minutes until the prawns are just pink. Add the noodles, beansprouts, egg, lime juice, fish sauce and sugar. Quickly toss together for 1 minute more until the egg is just cooked and everything is well mixed (you might want to use a pair of tongs to make this easier).
2 Remove from the heat, mix in most of the coriander leaves, then divide between two bowls. Scatter with the remaining coriander and the peanuts, and serve with lime wedges for squeezing over.

• Per serving 494 kcalories, protein 37g, carbohydrate 69g, fat 10g, saturated fat 2g, fibre 4g, sugar 9g, salt 2.91g

The fun of this fresh spicy soup is that everyone can add whatever they like to their own bowl. Don't hold back, as it's low in fat, too.

Mexican soup with chicken

2 tbsp olive oil
1 onion, chopped
4 garlic cloves, crushed
a pinch of dried chilli flakes
½ tsp ground cumin
400g can plum tomatoes
1.5 litres/2¾ pints chicken stock
2 skinless chicken breasts, sliced
(or use leftover cooked chicken)
juice of 2 limes

FOR THE TOPPINGS
tortilla chips, chopped avocado, lime wedges, red onion and coriander leaves

Takes 30 minutes • Serves 4

1 Heat the oil in a large pan. Add the onion and garlic, soften for 5 minutes, then stir in the chilli, cumin, tomatoes and chicken stock. Blitz in a food processor in batches, or use a hand blender to purée until smooth.
2 Return to the pan, then bring to the boil. If using raw chicken, add then reduce the heat and simmer for 10 minutes until cooked through. If using cooked, simply warm through. Stir in the lime juice and some seasoning, then ladle into bowls. Put the toppings in the middle of the table for everyone to help themselves.

• Per serving (soup only) 257kcalories, protein 34g, carbohydrate 10g, ffat 10g, saturated fat 1g, fibre 2g, sugar 6g, salt 2.12g

Here's a one-pan curry that both meat eaters and vegetarians will love. The texture of the aubergine plus the almonds in the creamy sauce makes it a really satisfying meat-free meal.

Aubergine and mushroom curry

3 tbsp olive oil
2 aubergines, each cut into about 8 chunks
250g/9oz chestnut mushrooms, halved
20g bunch of fresh coriander, stalks and leaves separated
2 large onions, quartered
a thumb-sized knob of ginger
3 garlic cloves, coarsely chopped
1 fat red chilli, seeded and half roughly chopped
1 tbsp each ground cumin and ground coriander
1 tbsp tomato purée
450ml/16fl oz vegetable stock
5 tbsp ground almonds
200g/8oz full-fat natural yogurt

Takes 30 minutes • Serves 4

1 Heat 2 tablespoons oil in a large frying pan, then fry the aubergines for 10 minutes until golden and soft. (The chunks will absorb all the oil at first, but keep cooking and it will be released again.) Add the mushrooms after 5 minutes; once golden, tip them out of the pan.
2 Meanwhile, whiz the coriander stalks, onions, ginger, garlic and chopped chilli to a paste in a food processor. Add 1 tablespoon oil to the pan, then fry the paste for 2 minutes.
3 Tip in the spices and tomato purée. Stir for 2 minutes, then return the aubergines and mushrooms. Tip in the stock, ground almonds and most of the yogurt. Simmer for 5 minutes until the sauce has thickened. Serve with slices of the remaining chilli, coriander leaves and a drizzle of the remaining yogurt.

• Per serving 307 kcalories, protein 11g, carbohydrate 20g, fat 21g, saturated fat 3g, fibre 7g, sugar 14g, salt 0.32g

Use up slightly stale bread to make the crunchy topping for this easy bake. Just a little chorizo goes a long way, keeping the dish low in fat but with a big, gutsy flavour.

Leek, butter bean and chorizo gratin

1 tbsp olive oil
75g pack chorizo, roughly chopped
4 large leeks, thinly sliced
3 garlic cloves, sliced
100ml/3½fl oz dry sherry
2 × 400g cans butter beans, drained and rinsed
450ml/16fl oz hot vegetable stock
85g/3oz bread, torn into pieces

Takes 35 minutes • Serves 4

1 Preheat the oven to 200°C/180°C fan/gas 6. Pour the oil into a baking dish, toss with the chorizo, leeks and half the garlic then bake uncovered for 10 minutes. Stir in the sherry, beans and stock, and return to the oven for 5 minutes. Season.
2 Meanwhile, blitz the bread to coarse crumbs with the remaining garlic. Scatter this over the chorizo, leek and bean mix, and bake for 10 minutes more until golden.

• Per serving 275 kcalories, protein 15g, carbohydrate 32g, fat 9g, saturated fat 2g, fibre 9g, sugar 7g, salt 2.41g

Turn your leftover chicken into a hearty soup, finished with a delicious fresh swirl of creamy lemon and garlic Greek yogurt.

Roast chicken soup

1 tbsp olive oil
2 onions, chopped
3 medium carrots, chopped
1 tbsp fresh thyme leaves,
roughly chopped
1.4 litres/2½ pints chicken stock
300g/10oz leftover roast chicken,
shredded and skin removed
200g/8oz frozen peas
3 tbsp Greek yogurt
1 garlic clove, crushed
squeeze of fresh lemon juice
crusty bread, to serve

Takes 40 minutes • Serves 4

1 Heat the oil in a large heavy-based pan. Add the onions, carrots and thyme, then gently fry for 15 minutes. Stir in the stock, bring to a boil, cover, then simmer for 10 minutes.
2 Add the chicken. Remove half the soup mixture and purée it with a stick blender. Tip back into the pan with the rest of the soup, the peas and some seasoning, then simmer for 5 minutes until hot through.
3 Mix together the yogurt, garlic and lemon juice. Swirl into the soup once spooned into bowls, then serve with crusty bread.

• Per serving 339 kcalories, protein 39g, carbohydrate 18g, fat 13g, saturated fat 3g, fibre 6g, sugar 11g, salt 2g

Add a mildly spicy twist to salmon with this satisfying
and smart one-pot.

Pepper-crusted salmon with garlic chickpeas

4 tbsp olive oil
2 garlic cloves, finely chopped
2 × 400g cans chickpeas, drained
and rinsed
150ml/¼ pint vegetable or fish stock
4 skinless salmon fillets, about
150g/5oz each
2 tsp black peppercorns,
roughly crushed
1 tsp paprika
zest and juice of 2 limes, plus
wedges to garnish
130g bag baby leaf spinach

Takes 25 minutes • Serves 4

1 Preheat the oven to 190°C/170°C fan/
gas 5. Heat 3 tablespoons oil in an ovenproof
pan, add the garlic, then gently cook for
around 5 minutes without browning. Add the
chickpeas and stock. Sit the salmon fillets
on top of the chickpeas, then scatter the
fillets with the pepper, paprika, lime zest and
some salt. Drizzle with the remaining oil. Bake
for 12–15 minutes until the salmon is just
cooked and the chickpeas are warmed
right through.
2 Lift the salmon off and keep warm. Put the
pan over a medium heat and lightly mash the
chickpeas using a potato masher. Fold in the
spinach leaves – they will quickly wilt. Season
with lime juice and salt and pepper. Serve
with the salmon, garnished with lime wedges.

• Per serving 531 kcalories, protein 41g, carbohydrate
23g, fat 32g, saturated fat 5g, fibre 6g, sugar 2g,
salt 1.01g

Mild spices and a rich tomato sauce make so much more of sausages.
The rice is cooked in the sauce and absorbs the tasty juices.

Fragrant pork and rice

4–6 good-quality sausages
1 tbsp olive oil
½ onion, finely chopped
2 garlic cloves, crushed
2 tsp each ground cumin
and coriander
140g/5oz long grain rice
850ml/1½ pints vegetable stock
400g can chopped tomatoes
½ × small bunch of fresh coriander,
leaves picked
crusty bread, to serve

Takes 40 minutes • Serves 4

1 Split the sausage skins, squeeze out the meat, then roll it into small meatballs, each about the size of a large olive. Heat the oil in a large non-stick pan, then brown the meatballs well on all sides until cooked – you might need to do this in batches. Set the meatballs aside.
2 Add the onion and garlic to the pan. Soften for 5 minutes, stir in the spices and rice, then cook for another minute. Pour in the stock and tomatoes. Bring to a simmer, scraping up any sausagey bits from the bottom of the pan. Simmer for 10 minutes until the rice is just cooked, then stir in the meatballs with some seasoning. Ladle into bowls, scatter with coriander and serve with crusty bread.

• Per serving 408 kcalories, protein 17g, carbohydrate 43g, fat 20g, saturated fat 5g, fibre 2g, sugar 6g, salt 1.56g

All the flavours of pork satay come together in this delicious stir-fry.
If your noodles look like they're sticking once drained, just add a few
drops of vegetable or sesame oil to the bowl and toss to coat.

Pork and peanut noodles

300g/10oz thin rice noodles
500g pack minced pork
1 garlic clove, crushed
250g pack mangetout
3 tbsp crunchy peanut butter
1 red chilli, seeded and
finely chopped
2 tsp light muscovado sugar
1 tbsp light soy sauce
1 small bunch of fresh coriander,
chopped, to garnish

Takes 20 minutes • Serves 4

1 Place the noodles in a large bowl and cover with boiling water. Leave to soak for 5 minutes, then drain and set aside.
2 Meanwhile, heat a wok or large frying pan and cook the pork mince over a high heat for 10 minutes, or until the juices have evaporated and the pork is starting to look crisp. Throw in the garlic and mangetout, and fry together for 2 minutes.
3 Whisk together the peanut butter, chilli, sugar and soy sauce in a bowl, then loosen with 2 tablespoons warm water. Add the noodles and peanut sauce to the pan, toss everything well, then fry for 1 minute, stirring until warmed through. Sprinkle over the coriander and serve in bowls.

• Per serving 551 kcalories, protein 33g, carbohydrate 68g, fat 18g, saturated fat 6g, fibre 2g, sugar 6g, salt 1.02g

Stack up the flavours in these big and bold chicken burgers.

Fully loaded Cajun chicken burgers

1 tbsp ground cumin
1 tbsp ground coriander
1 tbsp paprika
2 tbsp olive oil
4 skinless chicken breasts,
flattened a little
4 ciabatta rolls, split
4 rashers smoked bacon
2 avocados
mayonnaise, to spread (optional)
4 small handfuls of baby leaf spinach

Takes 35 minutes • Serves 4

1 Mix together the spices in a large dish with some salt and pepper and 1 tablespoon of the oil. Coat the chicken in the mix.
2 Heat a large frying pan, then toast the cut sides of the buns in the pan. Set aside. Heat the remaining oil in the pan then sizzle the chicken for 5 minutes on each side. Push to one side of the pan, then fry the bacon for a few minutes until cooked.
3 While the chicken is cooking, slice the avocados. To assemble the burgers, spread the buns with mayonnaise, if using, top with a handful of spinach, then a rasher of bacon. To keep the avocado in place, slice the chicken and place the avocado between the chicken slices. Top with the bacon and lastly the bun lid, press down lightly and serve.

• Per serving 721 kcalories, protein 51g, carbohydrate 51g, fat 36g, saturated fat 10g, fibre 5g, sugar 2g, salt 2.84g

If you've got time, this casserole will gently bubble away for up to 90 minutes; the meat becomes tender and falls away from the bones.

Honey mustard chicken pot with parsnips

1 tbsp olive oil
8 skinless chicken thighs, bone in
2 onions, finely chopped
350g/12oz parsnips, cut into sticks
300ml/½ pint vegetable stock
2 tbsp wholegrain mustard
2 tbsp clear honey
a few fresh thyme sprigs
flatleaf parsley, to garnish (optional)
steamed greens, to serve

Takes 45 minutes • Serves 4

1 Heat half the oil in a large frying pan or shallow casserole with a lid. Brown the chicken until golden, then set aside. Heat the remaining oil, then cook the onions for 5 minutes until softened.
2 Nestle the thighs back among the onions and add the parsnips. Mix the stock with the mustard and honey, then pour in. Scatter over the thyme, then bring to a simmer. Cover, then cook for 30 minutes (or longer) until the chicken is tender. Season and scatter with parsley, if using, and serve with steamed greens.

• Per serving 326 kcalories, protein 39g, carbohydrate 23g, fat 10g, saturated fat 2g, fibre 6g, sugar 15g, salt 0.82g

A honey glaze adds a lovely sweetness to a classic roast chicken; perfect against the tangy sweetness of roasted red onions.

Rosemary and balsamic chicken with roast onions

1 whole chicken, about 1.5kg/3lb 5oz
1 bunch of fresh rosemary
4 red onions, peeled and trimmed but left whole
3 tbsp olive oil
3 tbsp balsamic vinegar
1 tbsp clear honey

Takes about 2 hours • Serves 4

1 Preheat the oven to 190°C/170°C fan/gas 5. Starting at the neck, carefully loosen the breast skin away from the flesh. Place a sprig of rosemary down each side; put the rest in the cavity. Season the chicken, place in a roasting tin, then sit an onion in each corner of the tin. Drizzle the olive oil over everything then roast for 1 hour 20 minutes.
2 Meanwhile, stir the vinegar and honey together. After 40 minutes, take the chicken from the oven, drizzle the vinegar mix over the chicken and onions, then continue to roast.
3 At the end of the cooking time, remove the chicken from the tin, cover loosely with foil and set aside to rest for 20 minutes. Meanwhile, turn the onions over and continue to roast them until soft. Serve everything up with some of the sticky pan juices.

• Per serving 629 kcalories, protein 48g, carbohydrate 15g, fat 42g, saturated fat 11g, fibre 2g, sugar 12g, salt 0.44g

Create a smart plated dinner from just one pan
with this clever recipe.

One-pan duck with Savoy cabbage

2 duck breasts, skin on and scored
1 tsp black peppercorns, crushed
600g/1lb 5oz cooked new potatoes,
thickly sliced
1 bunch of flatleaf parsley,
roughly chopped
1 garlic clove, finely chopped
6 rashers smoked streaky bacon,
chopped
1 Savoy cabbage, trimmed,
quartered, cored and finely sliced
1 tbsp balsamic vinegar
2 tbsp olive oil

Takes 40 minutes • Serves 4

1 Generously season the duck skin with the peppercorns and a sprinkling of salt. Lay the duck skin-side down in a non-stick sauté pan, then place over a low heat. Leave for 15 minutes to brown and release its fat, then flip over on to the flesh side for 5 minutes.
2 Remove the duck from the pan, then turn up the heat. Add the potatoes to the pan, fry until brown and crisp, then scatter over the parsley and garlic. Scoop out with a slotted spoon on to a plate, then season with salt.
3 Keep the pan on the heat. Fry the bacon until crisp, then add the cabbage. Cook for 1 minute, add a splash of water, then fry for 2 minutes, just until the cabbage is wilted.
4 Meanwhile, mix any duck juices with the vinegar and oil. Slice the duck, serve with the cabbage and potatoes and top with a drizzle of dressing.

• Per serving 504 kcalories, protein 25g, carbohydrate 33g, fat 31g, saturated fat 8g, fibre 6g, sugar 7g, salt 1.16g

An elegant one-pan spring dish that looks and tastes very special.

Flambéed chicken with asparagus

4 skinless chicken breasts
1 tbsp seasoned plain flour
2 tbsp olive oil
a knob of butter
4 shallots, finely chopped
4 tbsp brandy or Cognac
300ml/½ pint chicken stock
16 asparagus spears, halved
4 rounded tbsp crème fraîche
1 tbsp chopped fresh tarragon
boiled new potatoes, to serve

Takes 45 minutes • Serves 4

1 Dust the chicken with the flour. Heat the oil and butter in a large, wide pan with a lid, add the chicken, then fry on all sides until nicely browned. Add the shallots, then fry for about 2 minutes until they start to soften, but not colour. Pour in the brandy, carefully ignite, then stand well back until the flames have died down. Stir in the stock and bring to the boil. Reduce the heat, cover, then cook for 15 minutes until the chicken is just tender.
2 Add the asparagus to the sauce. Cover, then cook for 5 minutes more until tender. Stir in the crème fraîche and tarragon, and warm through. Season to taste and serve with boiled new potatoes.

• Per serving 395 kcalories, protein 42g, carbohydrate 7g, fat 19g, saturated fat 8g, fibre 3g, sugar 4g, salt 0.9g

This full-flavoured chicken would make a great one-pan alternative to your usual weekend roast. Massaman curry paste is mild, so it's ideal for all the family.

Massaman curry roast chicken

1 whole chicken, about 1.8kg/4lb
2 thumb-sized knobs of ginger, 1 roughly chopped, 1 grated
1 lemongrass stick, bashed with a rolling pin
1 lime, cut into quarters
70g pack Massaman curry paste
1 tsp olive oil
450g/1lb baby new potatoes, any larger ones halved
400ml can coconut milk
1 tsp brown sugar (any type)
200g/8oz green beans, trimmed
1 tsp fish sauce
2 tbsp unsalted peanuts, crushed, to scatter

Takes 1 hour 40 minutes • Serves 4

1 Preheat the oven to 200°C/180°C fan/gas 6. Put the chicken in a medium roasting tin. Stuff the chopped ginger, lemongrass and half the lime into the cavity. Tie the legs together with string. Mix 1 teaspoon of curry paste with the oil, rub all over the chicken, then season.
2 Cover the chicken loosely with foil, then roast for 35 minutes. Uncover, add the potatoes and stir them around in any juices. Roast for 40 minutes more or until the chicken is cooked through and golden and the potatoes tender. Rest the chicken, loosely covered.
3 Meanwhile, add the remaining curry paste and the grated ginger to a pan and fry for 2 minutes. Stir in the coconut milk and sugar, and boil for 5 minutes until slightly thickened.
4 Tip in the beans. Simmer for 4 minutes, splash in the fish sauce, resting juices and a squeeze of lime and scatter with peanuts.

• Per serving 895 kcalories, protein 61g, carbohydrate 25g, fat 62g, saturated fat 27g, fibre 2g, sugar 7g, salt 1.75g

This is pure summer in a pan; simple to make and bursting with fresh Italian flavours.

Creamy pesto chicken with roasted tomatoes

4 skinless chicken breasts
3 tbsp pesto
85g/3oz mascarpone
4 tbsp olive oil
100g/4oz fresh breadcrumbs
(preferably from day-old bread)
175g/6oz cherry tomatoes on the vine
a handful of pine nuts
a handful of fresh basil leaves, to garnish
crusty bread, to serve

Takes 35 minutes • Serves 4

1 Preheat the oven to 200°C/180°C fan/gas 6. Use a small sharp knife to make a slit along the side of each chicken breast to form a pocket. Mix together the pesto and mascarpone, then carefully spoon a quarter of the mixture into each chicken breast and smooth over the opening to seal.
2 Brush a little oil, about 1 teaspoon, all over each chicken breast and season well. Tip the breadcrumbs on to a plate and season. Press each breast into the crumbs to coat. Place in a lightly oiled, shallow baking dish along with the tomatoes. Drizzle over the remaining oil.
3 Roast for 20–25 minutes until the chicken is golden and cooked through. Scatter over the pine nuts and cook for 2 minutes more. Sprinkle with basil leaves and serve with crusty bread.

• Per serving 545 kcalories, protein 40g, carbohydrate 22g, fat 33g, saturated fat 10g, fibre 1g, sugar 3g, salt 0.82g

If you haven't yet tried quinoa, give this a go. It's a filling grain that's super-good for you and cooks in the sauce just like rice would in a pilaf.

Spiced chicken balti

1 tbsp sunflower oil
2 large onions, thickly sliced
4 skinless chicken breasts
4 tbsp balti paste
200g/8oz quinoa
400g can chopped tomatoes
1 litre/1¾ pints chicken stock
50g/2oz roasted salted cashews
1 small bunch of fresh coriander,
leaves chopped

Takes 35 minutes • Serves 4

1 Heat the oil in a large pan, fry the onions for 5 minutes until golden and softened, then tip out on to a plate. Add the chicken breasts to the pan, browning them for a few minutes on each side, then stir in the balti paste, quinoa and onions. Sizzle for a few minutes, then pour in the tomatoes and stock, and give everything a good mix. Bubble for 25 minutes until the quinoa is tender and saucy.
2 Stir in the cashews and most of the coriander with some seasoning, then scatter over the rest of the coriander to serve.

• Per serving 527 kcalories, protein 47g, carbohydrate 45g, fat 19g, saturated fat 3g, fibre 5g, sugar 14g, salt 1.83g

The smoky chipotle chilli paste in this recipe can easily be swapped for harissa. Either way, it's a one-pan winner.

Smoky maple duck salad

2 duck breasts, skin on and slashed
3 tbsp maple syrup
1 garlic clove, crushed
1 tbsp chipotle chilli paste
160g bag bistro salad
1 bunch of radishes, about 200g/8oz,
thinly sliced or grated
1 tbsp sherry vinegar

Takes 30 minutes • Serves 2
(easily doubled)

1 Preheat the oven to 220°C/200°C fan/ gas 7. Place a roasting tin in the oven for 5 minutes. Season the duck well, then carefully put into the hot tin, skin-side down. Roast for 10 minutes until the skin is golden and crisp, and the fat has run out. (Or leave for 15 minutes if you prefer well done.)
2 Meanwhile, mix 2 tablespoons of the maple syrup with the garlic and chilli paste. Tip the fat out of the pan, turn the duck over, then roast for 5 minutes, basting with the maple mix once or twice until glazed and sticky. Remove and let the duck rest for 5 minutes.
3 Pile the salad and the radishes on to plates. Slice the duck; nestle it into the salad. Stir the rest of the maple syrup and the sherry vinegar into the pan juices, then drizzle over the salad to serve.

• Per serving 527 kcalories, protein 32g, carbohydrate 20g, fat 36g, saturated fat 10g, fibre 2g, sugar 18g, salt 0.54g

Big on flavour, easy on effort, this spicy chicken is just the thing for a busy weeknight supper.

Chicken with harissa and tomatoes

4 skinless chicken breasts
2 tsp harissa
1 tsp olive oil
1 tsp dried oregano
250g pack cherry tomatoes
a handful of pitted olives
(we used Kalamata)

Takes about 20 minutes • Serves 4

1 Preheat the oven to 200°C/180°C fan/gas 6. Put the chicken into a medium roasting tin, then rub with the harissa, oil and oregano. Cover with foil and roast for 5 minutes.
2 Remove the foil and add the cherry tomatoes and olives to the tray. Roast for 10 minutes more until the tomato skins start to split and the chicken is cooked through.

• Per serving 184 kcalories, protein 34g, carbohydrate 2g, fat 4g, saturated fat 1g, fibre 1g, sugar 2g, salt 0.41g

This one-pot recipe has an Italian theme running through it with the wine, pancetta and plum tomatoes. But although this is a pie, you don't have to make any pastry – there's not a rolling pin in sight.

Italian chicken and butternut pie

3 tbsp olive oil
8 large skinless chicken thigh fillets, quartered
130g pack cubed pancetta
1 large butternut squash, flesh cut into 2.5cm/1in cubes
1 large onion, thinly sliced
2 garlic cloves, thinly sliced
1 tsp dried marjoram
200ml/7fl oz Italian red wine
1 level tbsp plain flour
2 × 400g cans Italian plum tomatoes
2 tbsp redcurrant or cranberry jelly
1 garlic and herb or plain ciabatta, very thinly sliced
3 tbsp freshly grated Parmesan

Takes 1¼–1½ hours • Serves 6

1 Heat 2 tablespoons oil in a large casserole and lightly brown the chicken all over. Lift out of the pan, tip in the pancetta, squash and onion, and soften for 8 minutes, stirring occasionally. Return the chicken to the pan, add the garlic and marjoram and cook for 1 minute. Pour all but 2 tablespoons of the wine into the pan and bubble for 5 minutes.
2 Blend the flour with reserved wine until smooth. Stir into the pan with the tomatoes, jelly and seasoning. Lower the heat, half-cover, then simmer for 30–40 minutes until the squash is tender.
3 Preheat the oven to 220°C/200°C fan/gas 7. Lay the slices of ciabatta on top of the casserole, drizzle with the remaining olive oil, sprinkle with the Parmesan and some black pepper. Bake for 15 minutes or until golden.

• Per serving 491 kcalories, protein 41g, carbohydrate 42g, fat 16g, saturated fat 5g, fibre 4g, added sugar 2g, salt 2.17g

Anchovies are often used in Italian cooking to add a deeply savoury edge to a recipe. This is a great dish for the freezer.

Rosemary chicken with tomato sauce

1 tbsp olive oil
8 boneless skinless chicken thighs
1 fresh rosemary sprig, leaves finely chopped
1 red onion, finely sliced
3 garlic cloves, sliced
2 anchovy fillets, chopped
400g can chopped tomatoes
1 tbsp capers, drained
75ml/2½fl oz red wine, water or stock
crusty bread, to serve

Takes 35 minutes • Serves 4

1 Heat half the oil in a non-stick pan, then brown the chicken all over. Add half the chopped rosemary, stir to coat, then set aside on a plate.
2 In the same pan, heat the rest of the oil, then gently fry the onion for roughly 5 minutes until soft. Add the garlic, anchovies and remaining rosemary, then fry for a few minutes more until fragrant. Pour in the tomatoes and capers with the wine, water or stock.
3 Bring to the boil, then return the chicken pieces to the pan. Cover, then cook for 20 minutes until the chicken is tender. Season and serve with crusty bread.

• Per serving 275 kcalories, protein 44g, carbohydrate 5g, fat 9g, saturated fat 3g, fibre 2g, sugar 4g, salt 1.09g

Chicken thighs cook to melting softness and inject plenty of flavour into the stock in this vibrant and healthy herby casserole. They are also easier on the purse than breast meat.

Spring chicken in a pot

1 tbsp olive oil
1 onion, chopped
500g/1lb 2oz boneless skinless chicken thighs
300g/10oz small new potatoes
425ml/¾ pint low-salt vegetable stock
350g/12oz broccoli, cut into small florets
350g/12oz spring greens, shredded
140g/5oz petits pois
1 bunch of spring onions, sliced
2 tbsp pesto

Takes about 1 hour • Serves 4

1 Heat the oil in a large, heavy pan. Add the onion, gently fry for 5 minutes until softened, add the chicken, then fry until lightly coloured. Add the potatoes, stock and plenty of freshly ground black pepper, then bring to the boil. Cover, then simmer for 30 minutes until the potatoes are tender and the chicken is cooked through.
2 Add the broccoli, spring greens, petits pois and spring onions, stir well, then return to the boil. Cover, then cook for 5 minutes more, stir in the pesto and serve.

• Per serving 339 kcalories, protein 36g, carbohydrate 27g, fat 10g, saturated fat 3g, fibre 8g, sugar 12g, salt 0.5g

This is a great way to make a chicken go further. It takes some time, but is well worth it as you'll get every single bit of flavour from the bird.

Mustard chicken with winter vegetables

1 whole chicken, about 1.8kg/4lb
2 onions
6 celery sticks
6 carrots
2 bay leaves
2 fresh thyme sprigs
1 tsp black peppercorns
3 small turnips
50g/2oz butter
100g/4oz smoked bacon lardons
1 tbsp plain flour
2 tbsp wholegrain mustard
3 rounded tbsp crème fraîche
chopped fresh parsley, to serve

Takes 2 hours 40 minutes • Serves 4–6

1 Put the chicken in a casserole. Halve an onion, celery stick and carrot. Add to the pot with the herbs, peppercorns and some salt. Add water to halfway up the chicken, boil, then simmer, covered, for 1½ hours. Remove the chicken and strain the stock into a bowl. Chop all remaining veg.
2 Strip the chicken meat from the bones and tear into pieces. Heat the butter in a pan, add the onion and lardons; fry for 5 minutes. Add the remaining veg; fry for 2 minutes. Stir in the flour for 1 minute then add 900ml/1½ pints of the stock, topping up with water if need be. Simmer, covered, for 25 minutes until the vegetables are tender.
3 Add the chicken with the mustard and crème fraîche, simmer, stirring gently. Season and sprinkle with parsley before serving.

• Per serving 920 kcalories, protein 71g, carbohydrate 20g, fat 62g, saturated fat 23g, fibre 6g, sugar 14g, salt 3.06g

If you like the zesty, spicy flavours of Moroccan food, you'll enjoy this simple-to-make chicken dish. The couscous absorbs all the cooking juices, keeping in every bit of flavour.

Chicken and couscous one-pot

8 chicken thighs, skin on
and bone in
2 tsp ground turmeric
1 tbsp garam masala
2 tbsp sunflower oil
2 onions, finely sliced
3 garlic cloves, sliced
450ml/16fl oz chicken stock
a large handful of whole green olives
zest and juice of 1 lemon
250g/9oz couscous
1 small bunch of flatleaf parsley,
chopped

Takes 1 hour 10 minutes • Serves 4

1 Toss the chicken thighs in half the spices and a pinch of salt. Heat 1 tablespoon of the oil in a large pan. Fry the chicken, skin-side down, for 10 minutes, then turn and cook for 2 minutes more. Remove from the pan. Add the remaining oil then gently fry the onions and garlic for 8 minutes until golden. Stir in remaining spices for 1 minute. Add the stock, olives and chicken to the pan, skin-side up.
2 Cover, then simmer for 40 minutes. Lift the chicken on to a plate and keep warm. Off the heat, stir the lemon juice and couscous into the pan – add boiling water just to cover the couscous, if needed. Re-cover then let stand for 5 minutes until the couscous is soft. Fork half the parsley and lemon zest through the couscous, then sit the chicken on top. Scatter with the remaining parsley and zest.

• Per serving 900 kcalories, protein 60g, carbohydrate 42g, fat 56g, saturated fat 15g, fibre 2g, sugar 5g, salt 1.75g

This freezes really well, so why not make double
and freeze half for next time?

Chicken and white bean stew

2 tbsp sunflower oil
400g/14oz boneless skinless
chicken thighs, cut into chunks
1 onion, finely chopped
3 carrots, finely chopped
3 celery sticks, finely chopped
2 fresh thyme sprigs or ½ tsp dried
1 bay leaf, fresh or dried
600ml/1 pint vegetable or chicken
stock
2 × 400g cans haricot beans,
drained and rinsed
a little chopped fresh parsley
crusty bread, to serve

Takes 1 hour 20 minutes • Serves 4

1 Heat the oil in a large pan, add the
chicken, then fry until lightly browned. Add
the veg, then fry for a few minutes more. Stir
in the herbs and stock. Bring to the boil. Stir
well, reduce the heat, then cover and cook
for 40 minutes, until the chicken is tender.
2 Stir the beans into the pan, then simmer
for 5 minutes. Season to taste, stir in the
parsley and serve with crusty bread.

• Per serving 291 kcalories, protein 30g, carbohydrate
24g, fat 9g, saturated fat 2g, fibre 11g, sugar 9g,
salt 0.66g

It's really worth making your own Thai curries for their lively freshness of flavour. Duck makes an unusual and luxurious alternative to chicken.

French bean and duck Thai curry

3–4 duck breasts, about
700g/1lb 9oz in total
6 tbsp Thai green curry paste
1 tbsp light brown sugar,
plus extra to taste
400ml can coconut milk
2 tbsp fish sauce,
plus extra to taste
juice of 2 limes
6 kaffir lime leaves, 3 left whole and
3 finely shredded
200g/8oz French beans, trimmed
2 handfuls of beansprouts
a handful of coriander leaves
1 red chilli, seeded and sliced

Takes 2 hours • Serves 4

1 Place a deep frying pan over a low heat and add the duck breasts, skin-side down. Slowly fry until the golden and there's a pool of fat in the bottom; about 20 minutes. Flip on to the other side for 1 minute, then remove.
2 Pour all but 2 tablespoons of the fat from the pan. Fry the curry paste and sugar for around 1–2 minutes then tip in the coconut milk, a can of water, the fish sauce, half the lime juice and the whole lime leaves. Simmer, then slice the duck breasts and add to the curry. Cover, then cook very gently for 1 hour.
3 Add the beans, then simmer, covered, for 10 minutes. Add the remaining lime juice and a little more fish sauce or sugar to season. Stir in the beansprouts, cook for 1 minute more, then serve topped with coriander, the shredded lime leaves and sliced chilli.

• Per serving 638 kcalories, protein 28g, carbohydrate 11g, fat 57g, saturated fat 26g, fibre 2g, sugar 9g, salt 2.32g

This special dish can be relished by everyone, whether vegetarian or not. If you want to make it ahead, it will sit in the fridge, ready to bake, for a day or two.

Shallot tarte Tatin

2 tbsp olive oil
25g/1oz butter
500g/1lb 2oz shallots, peeled and halved
2 tbsp balsamic vinegar
1 tbsp fresh thyme leaves, or 2 tsp dried
300g/10oz puff pastry, defrosted if frozen and cut into two
100g/4oz grated Cheddar or Emmental

Takes 1 hour • Serves 4

1 Heat the oil and butter in a frying pan, add the shallots and fry gently for 10 minutes until softened and lightly browned. Stir in the vinegar, thyme and 1 tablespoon water; cook for 5 minutes, stirring occasionally. Tip into a shallow non-stick cake or pie tin, roughly around 20cm across. Leave to cool.
2 Preheat the oven to 200°C/180°C fan/ gas 6. Roll out each piece of pastry to about 5cm larger than the top of the cake tin. Put one piece over the shallots. Sprinkle evenly with cheese then cover with the second piece. Trim the pastry to a little larger than the tin, then tuck the edges down between the shallots and the side of the tin.
3 Bake for 25–30 minutes until the pastry is crisp and golden. Cool in the tin for around 5 minutes, turn out on to a flat plate, cut into wedges and serve warm.

• Per serving 510 kcalories, protein 13g, carbohydrate 33g, fat 37g, saturated fat 17g, fibre 2g, sugar 6g, salt 1.18g

Warm up lunchtimes with a bowl of gently spiced soup that's great with naan bread. If you're more into Italian flavours, try swapping the ginger and garam masala for 1 tablespoon of chopped rosemary.

Indian chickpea and vegetable soup

1 tbsp vegetable oil
1 large onion, chopped
1 tsp finely grated ginger
1 garlic clove, chopped
1 tbsp garam masala
850ml/1½ pints vegetable stock
2 large carrots, quartered lengthways and chopped
400g/14oz can chickpeas, drained and rinsed
100g/4oz green beans, chopped

Takes 30 minutes • Serves 4

1 Heat the oil in a medium pan, then add the onion, ginger and garlic. Fry for 2 minutes, then add the garam masala; give it 1 minute more, then add the stock and carrots. Simmer for 15 minutes, then add the chickpeas.

2 Use a stick blender to whiz the soup a little. Stir in the beans, simmer for 3 minutes, then divide into bowls and serve.

• Per serving 168 kcalories, protein 7g, carbohydrate 23g, fat 6g, saturated fat none, fibre 6g, sugar 10g, salt 0.66g

Take a handful of simple storecupboard ingredients and turn them into this hearty, comforting family supper. Little will they know that it's low in fat and includes three of their 5-a-day!

More-ish mushroom and rice

200g/8oz basmati rice
1 tbsp olive oil
1 large onion, chopped
2 tsp chopped fresh rosemary,
or 1 tsp dried
250g/9oz chestnut mushrooms,
quartered
2 red peppers, seeded
and sliced
400g can chopped tomatoes
425ml/¾ pint vegetable stock
chopped fresh parsley, to garnish

Takes 50 minutes • Serves 4

1 Preheat the oven to 190°C/170°C fan/ gas 5. Tip the rice into a sieve, rinse under cold running water, then leave to drain. Heat the oil in a flameproof casserole, add the onion, then fry until softened, which will take around 5 minutes.

2 Stir in the rosemary and mushrooms, then fry briefly. Add the rice, stir to coat in the oil, then tip in the peppers, tomatoes, stock and seasoning. Bring to the boil, stir, cover tightly with a lid, then bake for 20–25 minutes until the rice is tender. Scatter over the parsley and serve.

• Per serving 282 kcalories, protein 9g, carbohydrate 55g, fat 5g, saturated fat 1g, fibre 4g, sugar 7g, salt 0.36g

Food doesn't get much heartier, or fun to make, than this big, comforting cheese pie. Great with a simple salad.

Deep-dish cheese, onion and potato pie

200g/8oz strong hard cheese, ½ coarsely grated, ½ cut into small chunks
200g pot crème fraîche
500g/1lb 2oz shortcrust pastry
1kg/2lb 4oz floury potatoes, thinly sliced
2 onions, finely sliced
1 bunch spring onions, roughly chopped
a small pinch of grated nutmeg
a large pinch of paprika
1 egg, beaten

Takes 2 hours, plus resting time
Serves 6

1 Preheat the oven to 200°C/180°C fan/gas 6. Mix the grated cheese with the crème fraîche. Grease and lightly flour a pie dish or shallow cake tin about 23cm wide. Roll out two-thirds of the pastry on a floured surface until large enough to line the tin.
2 Layer the potatoes, onions and chunks of cheese with splodges of the crème fraîche mix, seasoning with some black pepper and the nutmeg and paprika as you go. The filling will come up way above the pastry.
3 Roll the remaining pastry so it fits over the filling. Brush the sides with egg, lay the pastry over, then trim with a knife. Crimp the sides, brush all over with egg then bake on a baking sheet for 30 minutes. Reduce the oven to 180°C/160°C fan/gas 4, then bake for 1 hour more. Rest the pie for 10 minutes, then slice.

• Per serving 820 kcalories, protein 20g, carbohydrate 73g, fat 52g, saturated fat 26g, fibre 5g, sugar 5g, salt 1.53g

Vietnamese food is known for its hot, sour, sweet and fresh herby flavours. You'll find all of them in this reviving bowlful to be enjoyed by itself or with rice.

Vietnamese veggie hotpot

2 tsp vegetable oil
a thumb-sized knob of ginger, shredded
2 garlic cloves, chopped
½ large butternut squash, peeled and cut into chunks
2 tsp soy sauce
2 tsp light muscovado sugar
200ml/7fl oz vegetable stock
100g/4oz green beans, trimmed and sliced
4 spring onions, sliced
chopped fresh coriander, to garnish

Takes 25 minutes • Serves 4

1 Heat the oil in a medium-sized lidded pan. Add the ginger and garlic, then stir-fry for about 5 minutes. Add the squash, soy sauce, sugar and stock. Cover, then simmer for 10 minutes.
2 Remove the lid, add the green beans, then cook for 3 minutes more until the squash and beans are tender. Stir the spring onions through at the last minute, then sprinkle with coriander.

• Per serving 75 kcalories, protein 2g, carbohydrate 13g, fat 2g, saturated fat none, fibre 3g, sugar 9g, salt 0.53g

Our butternut risotto is so satisfying – bags of flavour, two of your 5-a-day and just one pan to deal with.

Risotto with squash and sage

2½ tbsp olive oil
a handful of fresh sage leaves,
6 finely chopped,
the rest left whole
4 slices dried porcini mushrooms
2 litres/3½ pints hot low-salt
vegetable stock
1 onion, finely chopped
2 garlic cloves, finely chopped
2 fresh thyme sprigs
700g/1lb 9oz butternut squash,
peeled and cubed
350g/12oz carnaroli (or arborio) rice
100ml/3½fl oz dry white wine
a handful of flatleaf parsley, chopped
50g/2oz Parmesan, grated
2 tbsp light mascarpone

Takes 1 hour • Serves 4

1 Heat ½ tablespoon oil in a pan, fry the whole sage leaves for a few seconds until starting to colour. Drain on kitchen paper. Soak the mushrooms in the hot stock.
2 Heat 2 tablespoons oil in the cooled pan. Add the onion, garlic, chopped sage, thyme and squash; gently fry for 10 minutes. On a medium heat, tip in the rice. Stir for 3 minutes then add the wine and stir for 1 minute.
3 Stir in a ladleful of hot stock (leaving the porcini behind). Continue gradually adding and stirring until the rice is soft with a little bite and almost all the stock is used. Season.
4 Off the heat, add a splash more stock to the pan then scatter over the parsley, half the Parmesan and the mascarpone. Cover for 3–4 minutes then stir. Scatter with remaining Parmesan and the crisp sage leaves to serve.

• Per serving 517 kcalories, protein 15g, carbohydrate 85g, fat 15g, saturated fat 5g, fibre 5g, sugar 10g, salt 0.37g

Making pizza dough from scratch is so much easier than you might think and takes just minutes in the food processor.

Superhealthy pizza

100g/4oz each strong white and strong wholewheat flour
7g sachet easy-blend dried yeast
125ml/4fl oz warm water

FOR THE TOPPING
200g can chopped tomatoes, juice drained
a handful of cherry tomatoes, halved
1 large courgette, thinly sliced using a peeler
25g/1oz mozzarella, torn into pieces
1 tsp capers in brine, drained
8 green olives, roughly chopped
1 garlic clove, finely chopped
1 tbsp olive oil
2 tbsp chopped fresh parsley, to garnish

Takes 20 minutes • Serves 2

1 Mix the flours and yeast with a pinch of salt in a food processor fitted with a dough blade. Pour in the water and mix to a soft dough, then work for 1 minute. Remove the dough and roll out on a lightly floured surface to a round about 30cm across. Lift on to an oiled baking sheet.
2 Spread the canned tomatoes over the dough to within 2cm of the edge. Arrange the cherry tomatoes and courgette slices over the top, then scatter with the mozzarella. Mix together the capers, olives and garlic, then scatter over the top. Drizzle evenly with the oil. Leave to rise for 20 minutes. Preheat the oven to 240°C/220°C fan/gas 9.
3 Bake the pizza for 10–12 minutes until crisp and golden around the edge. Scatter with the parsley to serve.

• Per serving 479 kcalories, protein 19g, carbohydrate 78g, fat 13g, saturated fat 3g, fibre 10g, sugar 9g, salt 1.43g

This punchy dish can be prepared in advance. Cook until the end of step 2, then gently re-heat and crack in the eggs.

Easy ratatouille with poached eggs

1 tbsp olive oil
1 large onion, chopped
1 red or orange pepper, seeded and thinly sliced
2 garlic cloves, finely chopped
1 tbsp chopped fresh rosemary
1 aubergine, diced
2 courgettes, diced
400g can chopped tomatoes
1 tsp balsamic vinegar
4 large eggs
a handful of fresh basil leaves, to garnish
crusty bread, to serve

Takes 1 hour 20 minutes • Serves 4

1 Heat the oil in a large frying pan. Add the onion, pepper, garlic and rosemary, then cook for 5 minutes, stirring frequently, until the onion has softened. Add the aubergine and courgettes, then cook for 2 minutes more.
2 Add the tomatoes, then fill the can with water, swirl it around and tip into the pan. Bring to the boil, cover, then simmer for 40 minutes, uncovering after 20 minutes, until reduced and pulpy.
3 Stir the vinegar into the ratatouille, then make four spaces for the eggs. Crack an egg into each hole and season with black pepper. Cover, then cook for 2–5 minutes until the eggs are set as softly or firmly as you like. Scatter over the basil and serve with some crusty bread to mop up the juices.

• Per serving 190 kcalories, protein 12g, carbohydrate 13g, fat 11g, saturated fat 2g, fibre 5g, sugar 10g, salt 0.36g

Filled pasta such as tortellini freezes really well and only takes 1–2 minutes more to cook than it would unfrozen. Use all frozen veg, or vary the recipe by using asparagus or broccoli instead.

Springtime pasta

250g pack frozen ricotta and
spinach tortellini
50g/2oz frozen peas
50g/2oz frozen broad beans
1 tbsp olive oil
zest of 1 lemon
50g/2oz ricotta

Takes 10 minutes • Serves 2

1 Bring a pan of salted water to the boil. Tip in the pasta and cook for 3–4 minutes, then lift it out with a slotted spoon into a large bowl. Add the peas and broad beans to the pan, bring back to boil, then boil for 1 minute or until tender.
2 Drain well, then add to the pasta and toss through the olive oil and lemon zest. Place on plates, dollop over the ricotta and serve.

• Per serving 472 kcalories, protein 18g, carbohydrate 62g, fat 19g, saturated fat 8g, fibre 5g, sugar 5g, salt 1.34g

Mushrooms in a creamy sauce make the perfect quick fix, served on wholegrain toast. Choose chestnut mushrooms over white ones as they have a much deeper flavour.

Mushroom stroganoff on toast

25g/1oz ready-made garlic butter (or mix 25g/1oz butter with 1 crushed garlic clove), plus a little extra for spreading
250g pack chestnut mushrooms, thickly sliced
2 thick slices of granary bread
1 tsp wholegrain mustard
5 tbsp soured cream or crème fraîche
a few snipped fresh chives or spring onion tops

Takes 10 minutes • Serves 2

1 Tip the butter into a pan then, when sizzling, add the mushrooms and cook over a high heat, stirring occasionally until the mushrooms are tender and juicy.
2 Meanwhile, toast and lightly butter the bread and put on two plates. Stir the mustard and some salt and pepper into the mushrooms along with 4 tablespoons of the soured cream or crème fraîche. When lightly mixed, pile the mushrooms and their creamy sauce on the toast. Spoon the last of the soured cream or crème fraîche on top, snip over the chives or spring onions and grind over some black pepper.

• Per serving 322 kcalories, protein 8g, carbohydrate 21g, fat 24g, saturated fat 14g, fibre 3g, added sugar none, salt 1.08g

Summery tomato-based stews like this one are perfect to make ahead.
You could switch the chickpeas for butter or cannellini beans.

Roast summer vegetables and chickpeas

3 courgettes, thickly sliced
1 aubergine, cut into thick fingers
3 garlic cloves, chopped
2 red peppers, seeded and chopped into chunks
2 large baking potatoes, peeled and cut into bite-sized chunks
1 onion, chopped
1 tbsp coriander seeds
4 tbsp olive oil
400g can chopped tomatoes
400g can chickpeas, drained and rinsed
a small bunch of coriander, roughly chopped
hunks of bread, to serve

Takes 1 hour 10 minutes • Serves 4

1 Preheat the oven to 220°C/200°C fan/gas 7. Tip all the vegetables into a large roasting tin or flameproof dish and toss with the coriander seeds, most of the olive oil and some salt and pepper. Spread everything out in a single layer and roast for 45 minutes, tossing once or twice until the vegetables are roasted and brown round the edges.
2 Place the tin over a low heat and add the tomatoes and chickpeas. Bring to a simmer and stir gently. Season to taste, drizzle with the remaining olive oil and scatter over the coriander. Serve from the tin or pile into a serving dish. Eat with hunks of bread.

• Per serving 327 kcalories, protein 11g, carbohydrate 40g, fat 15g, saturated fat 2g, fibre 9g, sugar 13g, salt 0.51g

Make onions into a meal with a simple cheesy stuffing
and a salad on the side.

Cheesy baked onions

4 large onions, peeled
½ × 150g ball reduced-fat
mozzarella, roughly chopped
85g/3oz Cheddar, grated
2 tbsp olives, halved
50g/2oz roasted red peppers from a
jar, drained and roughly chopped
1 garlic clove, crushed
50g/2oz breadcrumbs
leaves from a few fresh thyme sprigs

Takes 35 minutes • Serves 4

1 Preheat the oven to 220°C/200°C fan/
gas 7. Halve each onion through the middle.
Microwave in a baking dish in pairs for around
4 minutes on High until soft. Remove the
middles of the onions, leaving about three
outer layers in place, like little bowls.
2 Whiz the onion middles in a food processor
until pulpy. Mix with the mozzarella, half of
the Cheddar, the olives, peppers, garlic,
breadcrumbs and most of the thyme, then
season well. Spoon the filling into the onion
cases and return to the baking dish. Sprinkle
with the remaining Cheddar and thyme, then
roast for 15 minutes until hot through and
lightly golden.

• Per serving 255 kcalories, protein 13g, carbohydrate
27g, fat 11g, saturated fat 6g, fibre 4g, sugar 12g,
salt 1.16g

You'll love the combination of fresh tastes and textures in this dish – the crunch from the veg, the smooth noodles and the soft tofu, combined with a sweet and spicy sauce.

Singapore noodles with tofu

140g/5oz firm tofu
2 tbsp sunflower oil
3 spring onions, shredded
1 small knob of ginger, finely chopped
1 red pepper, seeded and thinly sliced
100g/4oz mangetout
300g pack straight-to-wok thin rice noodles
100g/4oz beansprouts
1 tsp tikka masala curry paste
2 tsp reduced-salt soy sauce
1 tbsp sweet chilli sauce
roughly chopped fresh coriander and lime wedges, to garnish

Takes 25 minutes • Serves 2 (easily doubled)

1 Rinse the tofu in cold water, then cut into small chunks. Pat dry with kitchen paper. Heat 1 tablespoon of the oil in a wok or large frying pan, add the tofu, then stir-fry for around 2–3 minutes until lightly browned. Drain on kitchen paper.
2 Add the remaining oil to the wok and let it heat up. Tip in the spring onions, ginger, pepper and mangetout, then stir-fry for 1 minute. Add the noodles and beansprouts, then stir to mix. Blend together the curry paste, soy, chilli sauce and 1 tablespoon water, then add to the wok, stirring until everything is well coated in the sauce. Serve sprinkled with coriander, with lime wedges for squeezing over on the side.

• Per serving 392 kcalories, protein 12g, carbohydrate 57g, fat 15g, saturated fat 2g, fibre 4g, sugar 12g, salt 3.20g

Soup can be both satisfying and special, as this dish proves.

Spring vegetable soup with basil pesto

1 tbsp olive oil
2 leeks, washed and chopped
100g/4oz green beans, halved
1 large courgette, diced
1.2 litres/2 pints hot vegetable stock
3 vine-ripened tomatoes,
seeded and chopped
400g can cannellini beans,
drained and rinsed
1 nest vermicelli pasta,
about 25g/1oz
crusty bread, to serve

FOR THE PESTO
25g pack fresh basil
1 garlic clove, crushed
25g/1oz pistachio or pine nuts
25g/1oz Parmesan or vegetarian
Parmesan-style cheese, grated
2 tbsp olive oil

Takes 25 minutes • Serves 2
(easily doubled)

1 Heat the oil, then fry the leeks until softened. Add the green beans and courgette, then pour in the stock and season to taste. Cover and simmer for 5 minutes.
2 Meanwhile, make the pesto. Put the basil, garlic, nuts, cheese, oil and ½ teaspoon salt in a food processor, then blitz until smooth.
3 Stir the tomatoes, cannellini beans and vermicelli into the soup pan, then simmer for 5 minutes more until the veg are just tender.
4 Stir in half of the pesto. Ladle the soup into bowls and serve with the rest of the pesto spooned on top. Eat with chunks of crusty bread on the side.

• Per serving 594 kcalories, protein 27g, carbohydrate 56g, fat 31g, saturated fat 6g, fibre 16g, sugar 19g, salt 2.35g

Veggie-friendly dishes

Try something different and tuck into a plateful of beautifully simple fennel and tomatoes. Serve with some goat's cheese, if you like, and scoop the whole lot up with crusty bread.

Fennel with tomatoes and white wine

4 fennel bulbs
2 tbsp fruity olive oil
2 garlic cloves, crushed
a generous pinch of crushed
dried chilli
1 tbsp chopped fresh thyme leaves
4 ripe tomatoes, peeled and
roughly chopped
150ml/¼ pint dry white wine
100ml/3½fl oz vegetable stock
(a cube is fine)
a pinch of caster sugar (optional)
1 tbsp chopped flatleaf parsley,
to garnish

Takes 1 hour 20 minutes
Serves 2 as a main or 4 as a starter

1 Preheat the oven to 180°C/160°C fan/ gas 4. Trim the fennel and cut into quarters through the root. (You may need to cut larger ones in half, then into thirds so they all cook evenly.) Heat the oil in a roasting pan on the hob, add the fennel and cook until golden brown on all sides. Remove from the pan.
2 Fry the garlic, chilli and thyme for around 30 seconds, add the tomatoes and cook for a further 3 minutes. Add the wine and bring to the boil. Simmer for 1 minute, add the stock, bring back to the boil and simmer for 2–3 minutes.
3 Season the tomato mix, adding a pinch of sugar, if needed, then add the fennel and spoon the sauce over it. Cover with foil and cook in the oven for 1 hour or until the fennel is tender. Scatter with the parsley and serve.

• Per serving 110 kcalories, protein 2g, carbohydrate 6g, fat 6g, saturated fat 1g, fibre 4g, added sugar none, salt 0.2g

This filling and balanced salad really will hit the spot with lots of texture and taste – and that all-important spicy kick.

Mexican bean salad

4 eggs
2 avocados, peeled and stoned
2 × 400g cans beans (we used kidney beans and pinto beans), drained and rinsed
1 small red onion, finely sliced
1 large bunch of fresh coriander, leaves only, roughly chopped
250g punnet cherry tomatoes, halved
3 tbsp good-quality shop-bought dressing (try one with lime and coriander)
1 red chilli, seeded and finely sliced
½ tsp ground cumin

Takes 20 minutes • Serves 4

1 Lower the eggs into a pan of boiling water and boil for 6½ minutes, then cool under running water.
2 Slice the avocados and place them in a large bowl with the beans, onion, coriander and tomatoes. Tip in 3 tablespoons dressing, the chilli and cumin, and toss well.
3 Once the eggs are just warm, peel off the shells and cut into quarters. Nestle the eggs into the salad and serve straight away.

• Per serving 430 kcalories, protein 20g, carbohydrate 25g, fat 29g, saturated fat 3g, fibre 10g, sugar 6g, salt 1.61g

Add colour, crunch and a dollop of cheesy indulgence to your
weeknight pasta with this simple recipe.

Broccoli, walnut and blue cheese pasta

200g/8oz penne pasta
250g/9oz broccoli florets
2 tbsp olive oil
4 tbsp walnut pieces
100g/4oz creamy blue cheese, such
as dolcelatte, cubed
squeeze of fresh lemon juice, to taste

Takes 15 minutes • Serves 2

1 Cook the pasta according to the packet instructions and then, 4 minutes before the end of cooking, throw in the broccoli. Drain, keeping a cup of the cooking water, then set aside.

2 Heat the oil in the pan, then add the walnuts and fry gently for 1 minute. Add 4 tablespoons of the reserved cooking water to the walnuts. Stir in the cheese until it melts, season, then stir in the lemon juice to taste. Tip the drained pasta and broccoli into the sauce, toss well, then serve.

• Per serving 758 kcalories, protein 28g, carbohydrate 80g, fat 38g, saturated fat 12g, fibre 7g, sugar 6g, salt 0.82g

A warming winter twist on chilli con carne; perfect for bonfire night. It's made with chunks of braising steak instead of mince for a meltingly tender result.

Spicy beef stew with beans and peppers

3½ tbsp vegetable oil
1kg/2lb 4oz stewing beef, cut into chunks
1 onion, sliced
2 garlic cloves, sliced
1 tbsp plain flour
1 tbsp black treacle
1 tsp ground cumin
400g can chopped tomatoes
600ml/1 pint beef stock
2 red peppers, seeded and sliced
400g can cannellini beans, drained and rinsed
soured cream and fresh coriander, to garnish
crusty bread, to serve

Takes 3 hours • Serves 6–8

1 Heat 1 tablespoon oil in a large pan with a lid. Season the meat, then cook about one-third of it over a high heat for 10 minutes until browned. Tip on to a plate and repeat with 2 tablespoons oil and rest of the meat.
2 Add a splash of water and scrape the bottom of the pan. Add ½ tablespoon oil. Turn down the heat; fry the onion and garlic until softened. Return the meat to the pan, add the flour and stir for 1 minute. Add the treacle, cumin, tomatoes and stock. Bring to the boil, reduce the heat, cover, then simmer for 1¾ hours. Stir occasionally and check that the meat is covered with liquid.
3 Add the peppers and beans, and cook for a further 15 minutes. Serve in bowls, with a dollop of soured cream and sprinkling of coriander, and bread to serve.

• Per serving 400 kcalories, protein 43g, carbohydrate 18g, fat 18g, saturated fat 5g, fibre 4g, sugar 8g, salt 1.2g

You can offer this one-pot to just about anyone – kids and adults alike. The Puy lentils and pancetta make it a bit special, and everyone loves sausages.

Lincolnshire sausage and lentil simmer

1 tbsp vegetable oil
130g packet cubed pancetta or diced bacon
2 packets Lincolnshire pork or other good-quality sausages
2 onions, roughly chopped
1 large carrot, chopped
4 garlic cloves, roughly chopped
3 fresh rosemary sprigs
300g/10oz Puy lentils
900ml/1½ pints hot chicken stock
1 tbsp white wine vinegar
400g can chopped tomatoes
2 tbsp chopped flatleaf parsley, to garnish

Takes 1½ hours • Serves 6

1 Heat the oil in a large casserole or very large sauté pan with a lid. Add the pancetta or bacon and the sausages, and sizzle for 10 minutes, turning the sausages occasionally until nicely browned and sticky. Scoop the sausages out on to a plate.

2 Add the onions, carrot and garlic to the pancetta and continue to cook for 3–4 minutes until the onions soften. Return the sausages to the pan and add the rosemary, lentils, stock, vinegar and tomatoes, then season with salt and pepper. Bring to the boil and simmer rapidly for 5 minutes, then lower the heat, cover and simmer for 45 minutes, stirring every so often until the lentils are tender. Check the seasoning, scatter over the parsley and serve from the pan.

• Per serving 640 kcalories, protein 39g, carbohydrate 37g, fat 37g, saturated fat 13g, fibre 6g, added sugar none, salt 4.24g

To turn this recipe into a quick coq au vin, make it with chicken breasts, leaving them in the pan as the wine reduces.

Steak and sticky red-wine shallots

8 shallots, peeled and quartered
2 sirloin steaks, about 175g/6oz each
crushed black peppercorns, to taste
25g/1oz butter
4 tbsp balsamic vinegar
1 large glass red wine, about 175ml/6fl oz
150ml/¼ pint beef stock

Takes 25 minutes • Serves 2

1 Half-fill a frying pan with water. Boil; simmer the shallots for 2–3 minutes, then drain and set aside.

2 Season the steaks with a little salt and plenty of crushed peppercorns. Heat half the butter in the pan until sizzling, then cook the steaks for 3 minutes on each side for medium or until done to your liking.

3 Remove the steaks and keep warm. While they rest, add the remaining butter to the pan, throw in the shallots, then sizzle in the sticky pan until starting to brown. Add the balsamic vinegar and bubble for a few minutes. Add the wine and boil down until sticky, then add the beef stock and simmer until everything comes together. Spoon the shallots over the steaks and serve.

• Per serving 524 kcalories, protein 40g, carbohydrate 10g, fat 33g, saturated fat 16g, fibre 1g, sugar 10g, salt 1.87g

Come home to a bowl of this hearty soup on a cold winter's day.
Pearl barley plumps up as it cooks and thickens the soup beautifully.

Hearty lamb and barley soup

1 tsp olive oil
200g/8oz lamb neck fillet, trimmed of
fat and cut into small pieces
½ large onion, finely chopped
50g/2oz pearl barley
600g/1lb 5oz mixed root vegetables
(we used potato, parsnip and
swede, peeled and cubed)
2 tsp Worcestershire sauce
1 litre/1¾ pints lamb or beef stock
1 fresh thyme sprig
100g/4oz green beans (frozen are
fine), halved
granary bread, to serve

Takes 35 minutes • Serves 4

1 Heat the oil in a large pan. Season the lamb, then fry for a few minutes until browned. Add the onion and barley, then gently fry for 1 minute. Add the veg, cook for 2 more minutes, then add the Worcestershire sauce, stock and thyme. Cover, then simmer for 20 minutes.
2 When everything is cooked, spoon about a quarter of the soup into a blender or processor and whiz, then stir it back into the rest of the soup. Add the green beans, simmer for 3 minutes, then ladle the soup into bowls and serve with granary bread.

• Per serving 258 kcalories, protein 17g, carbohydrate 26g, fat 11g, saturated fat 4g, fibre 4g, sugar 12g, salt 1.48g

Rich, tomatoey and better than anything you can buy – a homemade rojan josh is just three simple steps away. For a rich beef curry, use chunks of braising steak instead.

One-pan rogan josh

2 onions, quartered
4 tbsp sunflower oil
4 garlic cloves, finely crushed
a thumb-sized knob of ginger, peeled and very finely grated
2 tbsp madras curry paste
2 tsp paprika
1 cinnamon stick
6 green cardamoms, bashed to break the shells
4 cloves
2 bay leaves
1 tbsp tomato purée
1kg/2lb 4oz lean leg of lamb, cut into generous cubes
150g/5oz Greek yogurt
chopped fresh coriander leaves, to serve

Takes 1 hour 40 minutes • Serves 6

1 Put the onions in a food processor and whiz until very finely chopped. Heat the oil in a large heavy-based pan, then gently fry the onion with the lid on, stirring every now and then, until it is really golden and soft. Add the garlic and ginger, then fry for 5 minutes more.
2 Tip the curry paste, all the spices, bay leaves and tomato purée into the pan. Stir well over the heat for about 30 seconds, then add the meat and 300ml/½ pint water. Stir to mix, turn down the heat, then add the yogurt.
3 Cover the pan, then gently simmer for 40 minutes–1 hour until the meat is tender and the sauce nice and thick. Serve scattered with coriander.

• Per serving 386 kcalories, protein 37g, carbohydrate 6g, fat 24g, saturated fat 9g, fibre 1g, sugar 3g, salt 0.54g

The trick with this classic one-pot is to use a cheap cut of meat, which means you'll skimp on price but not quality. Middle neck (neck fillets) or scrag end are both really flavoursome and perfect for braising.

Irish stew

1 tbsp sunflower oil
200g/8oz smoked streaky bacon, preferably in one piece, skinned and cut into chunks
900g/2lb stewing lamb, cut into large chunks
5 medium onions, sliced
5 carrots, cut into chunks
3 bay leaves
1 small bunch of fresh thyme
100g/4oz pearl barley
900ml/1½ pints lamb stock
6 medium potatoes, cut into chunks
a small knob of butter
3 spring onions, finely sliced, to garnish

Takes 2½ hours • Serves 6

1 Preheat the oven to 160°C/140°C fan/gas 3. Heat the oil in a flameproof casserole. Sizzle the bacon for 4 minutes until crisp. Turn up the heat, add the lamb and brown for 6 minutes. Remove with a slotted spoon. Add the onions, carrots and herbs to the pan, then soften for 5 minutes. Return the meat to the pan, stir in the pearl barley and stock, then bring to a simmer.

2 Sit the chunks of potato on top of the stew, cover, then braise in the oven, undisturbed, for about 1½ hours until the potatoes are soft and the meat is tender. Remove from the oven, dot the potatoes with butter, scatter with the spring onions and serve scooped straight from the dish.

• Per serving 627 kcalories, protein 49g, carbohydrate 44g, fat 30g, saturated fat 14g, fibre 5g, sugar 11g, salt 2.13g

All this needs is some crusty bread and perhaps a salad, and you're looking at a real feast. Orzo looks like large grains of rice, but is actually pasta. If you can't find it, use another small pasta, like trofie.

Greek lamb with orzo

1kg/2lb 4oz boned shoulder of lamb
2 onions, sliced
1 tbsp chopped fresh oregano,
or 1 tsp dried
2 cinnamon sticks, broken in half
½ tsp ground cinnamon
2 tbsp olive oil
400g can chopped tomatoes
1.2 litres/2 pints hot vegetable or
chicken stock
400g/14oz orzo
freshly grated Parmesan, to garnish

Takes about 3 hours • Serves 6

1 Preheat the oven to 180°C/160°C fan/gas 4. Cut the lamb into 4cm chunks, then spread over the base of a large, wide casserole dish. Add the onions, oregano, cinnamon sticks, ground cinnamon and olive oil, then stir well. Bake, uncovered, for around 45 minutes, stirring halfway.
2 Pour over the chopped tomatoes and stock, cover tightly, then return to the oven for 1½ hours, until the lamb is very tender.
3 Remove the cinnamon sticks, then stir in the orzo. Cover again, then cook for a further 20 minutes, stirring halfway through. The orzo should be cooked and the sauce thickened. Sprinkle with grated Parmesan and serve.

• Per serving 696 kcalories, protein 40g, carbohydrate 58g, fat 36g, saturated fat 16g, fibre 4g, sugar 7g, salt 0.68g

A superhealthy stew for all the family. The kids will enjoy the sweet flavours from the carrots and raisins, and everyone will love the warm, mild spices.

Pork ragout with carrots and cumin

1 tbsp olive oil
450g/1lb pork fillet, trimmed of all visible fat and cut into cubes
2 large onions, sliced
450g/1lb carrots, sliced thickly and diagonally
2 tsp ground cumin
½ tsp ground cinnamon
2 tbsp tomato purée
100g/4oz raisins
1 tbsp each toasted sesame seeds and chopped fresh coriander, to garnish
bread or rice, to serve

Takes 55 minutes • Serves 4

1 Heat the oil in a large pan, add the pork, then fry until the meat is sealed. Lift on to a plate. Add the onions, fry until lightly coloured, then stir in the carrots, spices, tomato purée and raisins. Add 450ml/16fl oz water, then bring to the boil.
2 Cover, gently cook for 25 minutes until the carrots are tender, add the pork to the pan, then simmer for 5 minutes until cooked through. Scatter over the sesame seeds and coriander, then serve with bread or rice.

• Per serving 328 kcalories, protein 28g, carbohydrate 34g, fat 10g, saturated fat 2g, fibre 5g, sugar 30g, salt 0.35g

The combination of lean lamb, couscous and carrot makes these burgers both nutritionally balanced and so satisfying.

Lighter lamb burgers with smoky oven chips

100g/4oz couscous
2 carrots, finely grated
250g pack extra-lean minced lamb
1 bunch of spring onions,
finely chopped
1 bunch of fresh mint, finely chopped
1 egg, beaten
rocket leaves and raita or natural
yogurt, to garnish

FOR THE SMOKY OVEN CHIPS
1 tbsp olive oil
750g/1lb 10oz sweet potatoes,
peeled and cut into chips
1–2 tsp smoked paprika

Takes 50 minutes • Serves 4

1 Preheat the oven to 200°C/180°C fan/gas 6. Place the couscous in a heatproof bowl and pour over 100ml/3½fl oz boiling water. Leave for a couple of minutes until all the liquid has been absorbed. Squeeze any liquid out of the carrots, then stir into the couscous along with the mince, spring onions, mint and egg. Season well and shape into four large burgers.
2 Pour the oil into a large, shallow non-stick baking sheet and heat in the oven. Add the sweet potato chips, stir around until coated with oil, then roast for 35 minutes.
3 After 15 minutes, add the burgers to the sheet. Ten minutes after this, sprinkle the paprika over the chips, shake to coat, then roast for 10 minutes more until the chips and the burgers are cooked through. Serve with the rocket and a dollop of the raita or yogurt.

• Per serving 400 kcalories, protein 19g, carbohydrate 58g, fat 12g, saturated fat 4g, fibre 6g, sugar 15g, salt 0.28g

This great little treat is easy to rustle up when you fancy something a bit special that won't take an age to put together.

Quick and creamy steak with onion

300g/10oz rump steak
1 tsp seasoned plain flour
a generous knob of butter
a drizzle of olive oil
1 red onion, finely chopped
175g/6oz chestnut mushrooms, sliced
2 tsp wholegrain mustard
142ml pot soured cream

Takes 30 minutes • Serves 2 (easily doubled)

1 Thinly slice the steak into long strips across the grain, trimming off any fat. Toss the strips in a teaspoon of seasoned flour.
2 Heat the butter and olive oil in a frying pan, then add the onion and fry for about 8 minutes, until softened and lightly coloured. Add the meat and quickly stir-fry until browned all over. Add the mushrooms and cook for 3 minutes, or until softened.
3 Season well with salt and freshly ground black pepper, then stir in the mustard and soured cream and bring to a gentle simmer, stirring, to make a smooth, creamy sauce.

• Per serving 502 kcalories, protein 38g, carbohydrate 9g, fat 35g, saturated fat 17g, fibre 2g, sugar 6g, salt 0.93g

Enjoy sausages without worrying about their fat content with this quick, full of flavour casserole.

Sausages with oregano, mushrooms and olives

450g pack reduced-fat sausages
1 tsp sunflower oil
2 tsp dried oregano
2 garlic cloves, sliced
400g can cherry or chopped tomatoes
200ml/7fl oz beef stock
100g/4oz pitted black olives
500g pack mushrooms, thickly sliced

Takes 30 minutes • Serves 4

1 Using kitchen scissors, snip the sausages into meatball-sized pieces. Heat a large pan and fry the pieces in the oil for about 5 minutes until golden all over.
2 Add the oregano and garlic, fry for 1 minute more, then tip in the tomatoes, stock, olives and mushrooms. Simmer for 15 minutes until the sausages are cooked through and the sauce has reduced a little.

• Per serving 264 kcalories, protein 20g, carbohydrate 12g, fat 16g, saturated fat 4g, fibre 4g, sugar 4g, salt 2.19g

The classic combination of pork and pineapple lives on in this slightly retro and irresistible sweet and sour one-pan dish.

Spiced pineapple pork

2 tsp vegetable oil
4 pork steaks, trimmed of excess fat
2 tbsp light muscovado sugar
1 tbsp dark soy sauce
1 tsp tomato purée
432g can pineapple rings in juice, drained but juice reserved
½ tsp chilli powder
1 tsp Chinese five spice powder
coriander leaves, to garnish

Takes 20 minutes • Serves 4

1 Add the oil to a large non-stick pan, season the steaks well, then fry for 5 minutes on each side until golden and almost cooked through. Mix together the sugar, soy sauce, tomato purée and most of the pineapple juice in a bowl.
2 Add the pineapple rings to the pan and let them caramelize a little alongside the pork. Add the chilli and five spice to the pan, then fry for 1 minute until aromatic. Tip in the soy mix and let it bubble around the pork and pineapple for a few minutes until slightly reduced and sticky. Sprinkle with coriander before serving.

• Per serving 315 kcalories, protein 39g, carbohydrate 22g, fat 9g, saturated fat 3g, fibre 1g, sugar 21g, salt 1.25g

A quick one-pan family roast that won't leave you arguing
about the washing up!

Rosemary roast chops and potatoes

3 tbsp olive oil
8 lamb chops
1kg/2lb 4oz potatoes, chopped into
small chunks
4 fresh rosemary sprigs
4 garlic cloves, left whole
250g/9oz cherry tomatoes
1 tbsp balsamic vinegar

Takes 40 minutes • Serves 4

1 Preheat the oven to 220°C/200°C fan/
gas 7. Heat half the oil in a flameproof
roasting tin or a shallow ovenproof casserole.
Brown the lamb for 2 minutes on each side,
then lift out of the pan. Add the rest of the oil,
throw in the potatoes and fry for 4–5 minutes
until starting to brown. Toss in the rosemary
and garlic, then nestle the lamb in along with
the potatoes.
2 Roast everything together for 20 minutes,
then scatter over the tomatoes and drizzle
with the vinegar. Place back in the oven
for 5 minutes until the tomatoes just begin
to split. Remove from the oven and serve
straight from the dish.

• Per serving 754 kcalories, protein 36g, carbohydrate
46g, fat 48g, saturated fat 21g, fibre 4g, sugar 4g,
salt 0.34g

You could use lamb chops for this recipe, if you prefer.
Simply trim the excess fat off the chops before browning.

Coddled pork with cider

a small knob of butter
2 pork loin chops
4 rashers smoked bacon,
cut into pieces
1 carrot, cut into large chunks
2 potatoes, cut into chunks
½ small swede, cut into chunks
¼ large cabbage, cut into
smaller wedges
1 bay leaf
100ml/3½fl oz cider
100ml/3½fl oz chicken stock

Takes 35 minutes • Serves 2
(easily doubled)

1 Heat the butter in a casserole dish until sizzling, then fry the pork for 2–3 minutes on each side until browned. Remove from the pan. Tip the bacon, carrot, potatoes and swede into the pan, then gently fry until slightly coloured.

2 Stir in the cabbage, sit the chops back on top, add the bay leaf, then pour over the cider and stock. Cover the pan, then leave everything to simmer gently for 20 minutes until the pork is cooked through and the vegetables are tender. Serve at the table spooned straight from the dish.

• Per serving 717 kcalories, protein 44g, carbohydrate 37g, fat 44g, saturated fat 17g, fibre 12g, sugar 20g, salt 2.59g

All these need is some crusty bread – though they're especially delicious with a spoonful of cranberry jelly or sauce.

Classic Swedish meatballs

400g/14oz lean minced pork
1 egg, beaten
1 small onion, finely chopped or grated
85g/3oz fresh white breadcrumbs
1 tbsp finely chopped fresh dill, plus extra to garnish
1 tbsp each olive oil and butter
2 tbsp plain flour
400ml/14fl oz hot beef stock

Takes 35 minutes • Serves 4

1 In a bowl, mix the mince with the egg, onion, breadcrumbs, dill and seasoning. Form into small meatballs about the size of walnuts – you should get about 20.
2 Heat the olive oil in a large non-stick frying pan and brown the meatballs. You may have to do this in two batches. Remove from the pan, melt the butter, then sprinkle over the flour and stir well. Cook for 2 minutes, then slowly whisk in the stock. Keep whisking until it is a thick gravy, then return the meatballs to the pan and heat through. Sprinkle with dill and serve.

• Per serving 301 kcalories, protein 26g, carbohydrate 22g, fat 13g, saturated fat 4g, fibre 1g, sugar 2g, salt 1.73g

This is a basic, economical but still completely delicious one-pan supper. Serve with plenty of ketchup, Worcestershire or brown sauce.

Corned beef hash

4 tbsp vegetable oil
900g–1kg/2–2¼lb large potatoes, cut into small chunks
a knob of butter
1 large onion, roughly chopped
340g can corned beef, cut into chunks

Takes 50 minutes • Serves 4

1 Heat 2 tablespoons oil in a large non-stick frying pan, then fry the potatoes for 5 minutes, stirring often. Add a cup of water to the pan and let it boil and bubble off for 5 minutes more until the potatoes are just tender. Tip out on to a plate.

2 Put the butter and 1 tablespoon more oil into the pan over a high heat. Once foaming, tip in the onion and cook for 5 minutes until golden. Pour in the remaining oil, turn up the heat then tip in the potatoes and corned beef. Season.

3 Cook for 15 minutes, folding and turning the hash every 2–3 minutes until you get lots of golden crispy bits. Reduce the heat halfway to medium–low; cook for 5 minutes more, folding and turning the hash every so often. Season, then serve from the pan.

• Per serving 487 kcalories, protein 28g, carbohydrate 42g, fat 24g, saturated fat 7g, fibre 4g, added sugar none, salt 2.14g

One-pots can be so good for you; this stew counts as three of your 5-a-day and it's low in fat.

Rich paprika seafood bowl

2 tbsp olive oil
2 onlons, halved and thinly sliced
2 celery sticks, finely chopped
1 large bunch of flatleaf parsley, leaves and stalks separated
2–3 tsp paprika
200g/8oz roasted red peppers from a jar, drained weight, thickly sliced
400g can chopped tomatoes with garlic
400g/12oz white fish fillet, cut into very large chunks
a few fresh mussels (optional)
lightly toasted bread, to serve

Takes 30 minutes • Serves 4

1 Heat half the oil in a pan, then add the onions, celery and a little salt. Cover, then gently fry until soft, about 10 minutes.
2 Put the parsley stalks, half the leaves, remaining oil and seasoning into a food processor, and whiz to a paste. Add this and the paprika to the softened onions, frying for a few minutes. Tip in the peppers and tomatoes with a splash of water, then simmer for 10 minutes until the sauce has reduced.
3 Lay the fish and mussels, if using, on top of the sauce, put a lid on, then simmer for 5 minutes until the fish is just flaking and the mussels have opened – discard any that stay shut. Gently stir the seafood into the sauce, season, then serve in bowls with some lightly toasted bread.

• Per serving 192 kcalories, protein 22g, carbohydrate 12g, fat 7g, saturated fat 1g, fibre 4g, sugar 8g, salt 1.14g

This is a popular way to serve fish in Thailand. The only difference is they deep-fry the fish; here we've kept everything in one pan.

Tilapia in Thai sauce

4 tilapia fillets (or choose any sustainably caught white fish)
2 tbsp cornflour
2 tbsp sunflower oil
4 spring onions, sliced
2 garlic cloves, crushed
a small knob of ginger, finely chopped
2 tbsp soy sauce
1 tbsp brown sugar
juice of 1 lime, plus 1 lime chopped into wedges, to serve
1 red chilli, seeded and sliced and a handful of Thai basil or coriander leaves, to garnish

Takes 30 minutes • Serves 2

1 Coat the fish fillets in the cornflour, then set aside. Heat the oil in a large non-stick frying pan, sizzle the fillets for 2–3 minutes on each side until crisp, then remove and keep warm.
2 In the same pan, briefly fry the spring onions, garlic and ginger, then add the soy sauce, brown sugar and lime juice, and simmer until slightly syrupy. Spoon the sauce over the fish, scatter with the chilli and Thai basil or coriander, then serve with the lime wedges on the side.

• Per serving 328 kcalories, protein 28g, carbohydrate 25g, fat 14g, saturated fat 2g, fibre 1g, sugar 10g, salt 2.94g

This cabbage stew is based on a peasant dish from south-west France and is served with everything from duck to fish.

Savoy cabbage and beans with white fish

a small knob of butter
5 rashers smoked streaky bacon, chopped
1 onion, finely chopped
2 celery sticks, diced
2 carrots, diced
1 small bunch of fresh thyme
1 Savoy cabbage, shredded
4 tbsp white wine
300ml/½ pint chicken stock
410g can flageolet beans in water, drained and rinsed

FOR THE FISH
2 tbsp olive oil
4 fillets sustainably caught white fish, each about 140g/5oz, skin on
2 tbsp plain flour

Takes 50 minutes • Serves 4

1 Heat the butter in a large non-stick frying pan until starting to sizzle, add the bacon, then fry for a few minutes. Add the onion, celery and carrots and cook for 8–10 minutes until softening, but not brown. Stir in the thyme and cabbage, then cook for a few minutes until the cabbage starts to wilt. Pour in the wine, simmer until evaporated, then add the stock and beans. Season, cover the pan, then simmer gently for 10 minutes until the cabbage is soft but still vibrant. Spoon the cabbage into serving bowls and keep warm.
2 Wipe out the pan and heat the oil in it. Season each fillet, then dust the skin with flour. Fry the fish, skin-side down, for 4 minutes until crisp, then flip over and finish on the flesh side until cooked through. Serve each fish fillet on top of the cabbage and beans.

• Per serving 423 kcalories, protein 42g, carbohydrate 29g, fat 16g, saturated fat 4g, fibre 10g, sugar 13g, salt 1.45g

So few ingredients, yet this dish really performs. The soy sauce adds a deep, savoury flavour to the tomatoes.

Tomato and thyme cod

1 tbsp olive oil
1 onion, chopped
400g can chopped tomatoes
1 heaped tsp light brown soft sugar
a few fresh thyme sprigs,
leaves stripped
1 tbsp soy sauce
4 sustainably caught white fish fillets

Takes 20 minutes • Serves 4

1 Heat the oil in a frying pan, add the onion, then fry for 5–8 minutes until lightly browned. Stir in the tomatoes, sugar, thyme and soy sauce, then bring to the boil. Simmer for 5 minutes, then slip the fish into the sauce.
2 Cover and gently cook for 8–10 minutes until the cod flakes easily.

• Per serving 172 kcalories, protein 27g, carbohydrate 7g, fat 4g, saturated fat 1g, fibre 1g, sugar 6g, salt 1.1g

Smoked salmon is no more costly than cooking with red meat and adds a touch of luxury to this simple weeknight supper.

Smoked salmon and lemon risotto

1 onion, finely chopped
2 tbsp olive oil
350g/12oz risotto rice,
such as arborio
1 garlic clove, finely chopped
1½ litres/2¾ pints boiling
vegetable stock
170g pack smoked salmon,
three-quarters chopped
85g/3oz reduced-fat mascarpone
3 tbsp flatleaf parsley, chopped
grated zest of 1 lemon, plus squeeze
of juice (optional), to taste
a handful of rocket leaves, to serve

Takes 25 minutes • Serves 4

1 Fry the onion in the oil over a medium heat for 5 minutes. Add the rice and garlic, then cook for 2 minutes, stirring continuously. Pour in the stock a ladleful at a time, stirring, until almost all the stock has been absorbed and the rice is cooked and creamy.
2 Remove from the heat and add the chopped salmon, mascarpone, parsley and lemon zest. Grind in some black pepper, but don't add salt as the salmon will be salty enough. Leave for 5 minutes to settle, then taste and add a little lemon juice, if you like. Serve topped with the reserved salmon (roughly torn) and some rocket leaves.

• Per serving 500 kcalories, protein 21g, carbohydrate 75g, fat 15g, saturated fat 5g, fibre 4g, sugar 5g, salt 2.58g

Pressing a layer of breadcrumbs on to fish not only adds crunch but also helps to cook it to perfection, protecting it from the direct heat of the grill. The crumbs can be made using any green herbs.

Lemon and rosemary crusted fish fillets

4 sustainably caught white fish fillets
2 fresh rosemary sprigs, leaves chopped, or 1 tsp dried
50g/2oz bread (about 2 slices), torn into pieces
zest of 2 lemons, plus wedges to serve
1 tbsp olive oil

Takes 20 minutes • Serves 4

1 Heat the grill to medium. Place the fish fillets, skin-side up, on a baking sheet, then grill for 4 minutes.
2 Meanwhile, place the rosemary, bread, lemon zest and some seasoning in a food processor, then blitz to make fine crumbs.
3 Turn the fish over, then press the crumbs over the top of each fillet. Drizzle with olive oil, then grill for 4 minutes until the crust is golden and the fish is cooked through and just flaking. Serve with lemon wedges for squeezing over.

• Per serving 184 kcalories, protein 26g, carbohydrate 6g, fat 6g, saturated fat 1g, fibre none, sugar none, salt 0.51g

Trout is quick and easy to cook, and makes a great heart-healthy meal. Swap for salmon, if you like; the cooking times will be the same.

Trout with almonds and red peppers

1 large red pepper, seeded and chopped
2 large tomatoes, roughly chopped, or a handful of cherry tomatoes, halved
1 garlic clove, chopped
1 tbsp olive oil, plus a little extra
1 tbsp balsamic vinegar
2 trout fillets, about 140g/5oz each
2 tbsp flaked almonds
lemon wedges and rocket leaves, to serve

Takes 40 minutes • Serves 2

1 Preheat the oven to 190°C/170°C fan/gas 5. Tip the pepper, tomatoes, garlic, oil and vinegar into a roasting tin, then toss them together. Roast for 20 minutes, then make a space in the roasting tin for the trout fillets, scattering with the almonds and a little salt and pepper.
2 Return the tin to the oven for a further 10–15 minutes, until the fish is cooked and the almonds lightly toasted. Serve with lemon wedges for squeezing over and rocket on the side.

• Per serving 326 kcalories, protein 31g, carbohydrate 11g, fat 18g, saturated fat 3g, fibre 3g, sugar 11g, salt 0.24g

Take the time to cook yourself something special, with this full-flavoured meal for one.

Smoked haddock with colcannon and mustard

200ml/7fl oz vegetable stock
1 medium potato, peeled and
chopped into small chunks
a large handful of kale, spring greens
or cabbage, finely shredded
a small knob of butter
140g/5oz piece smoked skinned
haddock (undyed is best)
1 heaped tbsp Dijon mustard
25g/1oz melted butter

Takes 30–40 minutes • Serves 1
(easily doubled)

1 Put the stock and potato in a small pan. Cover and boil for 6 minutes until the potato starts to fluff round the edges and the stock has reduced slightly. Throw in the greens and butter, stir, then cover the pan again, lower the heat and simmer for 4 minutes to soften the kale.
2 Lay the haddock fillet on top of the kale and potatoes, cover the pan and leave to steam gently for 5 minutes. Meanwhile, whisk the mustard, a splash of water and seasoning into the butter. Set aside.
3 Prod a corner of the haddock fillet – it's ready when it flakes easily. Lift out the cooked haddock and put it to one side. Mash the potato and kale together in the pan with the pan juices. Scoop the mash on to a warmed plate, sit the haddock on top and spoon the sauce over.

• Per serving 459 kcalories, protein 34g, carbohydrate 21g, fat 27g, saturated fat 15g, fibre 3g, added sugar none, salt 6.21g

Welcome in the first of the asparagus with this fresh one-pan recipe. It's really two recipes in one – for an easy side dish to complement a spring roast, just cook it without the fish.

One-pan salmon with roast asparagus

400g/14oz new potatoes, halved if large
2 tbsp olive oil
8 asparagus spears, trimmed and halved
2 handfuls of cherry tomatoes
1 tbsp balsamic vinegar
2 salmon fillets, about 140g/5oz each
a handful of fresh basil leaves, to garnish

Takes 1 hour 20 minutes • Serves 2

1 Preheat the oven to 220°C/200°C fan/gas 7. Tip the potatoes and 1 tablespoon of olive oil into an ovenproof dish, then roast the potatoes for 20 minutes until just starting to brown.

2 Toss the asparagus in with the potatoes, then return to the oven for 15 minutes. Throw in the cherry tomatoes and vinegar, and nestle the salmon amongst the vegetables. Drizzle with the remaining oil and return to the oven for a final 10–15 minutes until the salmon is cooked through. Scatter over the basil leaves and serve everything scooped straight from the dish.

• Per serving 483 kcalories, protein 33g, carbohydrate 34g, fat 25g, saturated fat 4g, fibre 3g, sugar 6g, salt 0.24g

One you've tried this can't-go-wrong curry you'll make it again and again. Frozen prawns are better value and are often in better condition than fresh.

Easy Thai prawn curry

1 tbsp vegetable oil
1 onion, chopped
1 tsp grated ginger
1–2 tsp Thai red curry paste
400g can chopped tomatoes
50g sachet creamed coconut
400g/14oz frozen raw peeled prawns
chopped fresh coriander leaves,
to garnish

Takes 20 minutes • Serves 4

1 Heat the oil in a medium saucepan. Tip in the onion and ginger, then cook for a few minutes until softened. Stir in the curry paste, then cook for 1 minute more. Pour over the chopped tomatoes and stir in the creamed coconut. Bring to the boil, then leave to simmer for 5 minutes, adding a little boiling water if the mixture gets too thick.
2 Tip in the prawns, then cook for around 5–10 minutes more, depending on how large they are. Sprinkle with coriander to serve.

• Per serving 180 kcalories, protein 20g, carbohydrate 6g, fat 9g, saturated fat 4g, fibre 1g, sugar 5g, salt 0.86g

This makes a wonderful end-of-week supper to share. The sherry adds steam to the pan and cooks the potatoes.

Friday-night fish with chorizo and new potatoes

1 tbsp extra-virgin olive oil, plus extra to serve
50g/2oz chorizo, peeled and thinly sliced
450g/1lb salad or new potatoes, sliced (we used Charlotte)
4 tbsp dry sherry (more if you need it)
2 skinless thick fillets white fish (we used sustainably caught haddock)
a good handful of cherry tomatoes, halved
20g pack flatleaf parsley, leaves chopped
crusty bread, to serve

Takes 30 minutes • Serves 2

1 Heat a large lidded frying pan, then add the oil. Tip in the chorizo, fry for 2 minutes until it starts to release its oils, then tip in the potatoes and some seasoning. Splash over 3 tablespoons sherry, cover the pan tightly, then leave to cook for 10–15 minutes until the potatoes are just tender. Move them around the pan a bit halfway through.
2 Season the fish well. Give the potatoes another stir, add the cherry tomatoes and most of the chopped parsley to the pan, then lay the fish on top. Splash over 1 tablespoon sherry, put the lid on again, then leave to cook for 5 minutes, or until the fish has turned white and is flaky when prodded in the middle. Scatter the whole dish with a little more parsley and drizzle with more extra-virgin oil. Serve straight away with crusty bread.

• Per serving 534 kcalories, protein 47g, carbohydrate 39g, fat 19g, saturated fat 4g, fibre 3g, sugar 5g, salt 0.79g

Use any sustainably caught white fish or salmon fillets in this recipe
– perfect mopped up with crusty bread.

One-pan Spanish fish stew

a handful of flatleaf parsley leaves,
chopped
zest and juice of 1 lemon
2 garlic cloves, finely chopped
3 tbsp olive oil, plus extra to drizzle
1 medium onion, finely sliced
500g/1lb 2oz floury potatoes, cut
into small cubes
1 tsp paprika
a pinch of cayenne pepper
400g can chopped tomatoes
1 fish stock cube, crumbled
200g/8oz raw peeled king prawns
½ × 410g can chickpeas,
drained and rinsed
500g/1lb 2oz skinless fish fillets, cut
into very large chunks

Takes 50 minutes • Serves 4

1 In a small bowl, mix the parsley with the lemon zest and half the garlic, then set aside. Heat 2 tablespoons oil in a large sauté pan. Add the onion and potatoes, cover and cook for 5 minutes until the onion has softened. Add the remaining oil and garlic and the spices, then cook for 2 minutes more.
2 Pour over the lemon juice, sizzle for a few seconds, then add the tomatoes, half a can of water and the stock cube. Season, cover, and simmer for 15–20 minutes until the potatoes are just cooked.
3 Stir through the prawns and chickpeas, then nestle the fish into the top of the stew. Reduce the heat, re-cover, then cook for about 8 minutes, stirring very gently once or twice. Scatter with the parsley mix and drizzle with a little olive oil to serve.

• Per serving 382 kcalories, protein 39g, carbohydrate 33g, fat 11g, saturated fat 2g, fibre 5g, sugar 5g, salt 1.92g

For this dish, try to buy the smallest mussels you can find;
they will always be the sweetest.

Steamed mussels with leeks, thyme and bacon

750g/1lb 10oz mussels
25g/1oz butter
6 rashers smoked streaky bacon,
chopped into small pieces
2 small leeks, sliced on the diagonal
a handful of fresh thyme sprigs
1 small glass cider or white wine
crusty bread, to serve

Takes 35 minutes • Serves 2

1 Scrub and de-beard the mussels. Heat half the butter in a pan, then sizzle the bacon for 3–4 minutes until starting to brown. Add the leeks and thyme, then gently fry everything together for 4–5 minutes until soft.
2 Turn the heat up high, add the mussels and cider or wine, then cover and cook for 4–5 minutes, shaking the pan occasionally, until the mussels have opened. Discard any that don't open.
3 Scoop the mussels and the other solid bits into a dish, then place the pan back on the heat. Boil the juices for 1 minute with the rest of the butter, then pour over the mussels and serve with crusty bread.

• Per serving 377 kcalories, protein 24g, carbohydrate 9g, fat 26g, saturated fat 12g, fibre 2g, sugar 5g, salt 2.76g

Medium or thick udon-style noodles work best in this recipe.
Serve with a spoon so you can slurp up all the soupy stock.

Super-fast prawn noodles

1 litre/1¾ pints chicken stock
2 tbsp oyster sauce
2 tbsp hoisin sauce
1 tbsp fish sauce
a large knob of ginger, shredded into thin matchsticks
300g/10oz peeled king prawns (raw would be best, but cooked are fine)
4 bok choi, each cut into quarters
2 sachets straight-to-wok noodles
4 spring onions, finely sliced, to garnish

Takes 15 minutes • Serves 4

1 In a wok or large pan, bring the stock to the boil. Stir the sauces into the stock, then add the ginger. Simmer for a moment, then add the prawns; if raw, simmer for 2 minutes until they turn pink before adding the bok choi; if cooked, add together with the bok choi and cook for 2 minutes until just wilted.
2 Slip the noodles into the broth and stir them gently to loosen. Bring the liquid back to a simmer and cook for 2 minutes more to warm them through. Scatter with spring onions and serve straight from the wok, using tongs for the noodles and a ladle for the broth.

• Per serving 277 kcalories, protein 29g, carbohydrate 33g, fat 4g, saturated fat none, fibre 2g, sugar 6g, salt 3.82g

Roasting is a foolproof way of cooking fish. In this recipe the fish stays moist and the peppers become soft and sweet.

Zesty roast salmon and cod

800g/1lb 12oz thick skinless salmon fillet, cut into 8
800g/1lb 12oz thick skinless sustainably caught cod loin, cut into 8
85g/3oz raisins
3 tbsp olive oil
zest and juice of 2 oranges
3 red peppers, halved, seeded and cut into 6
3 orange peppers, halved, seeded and cut into 6
50g/2oz toasted pine nuts
a large handful of flatleaf parsley, roughly chopped, to garnish

Takes about 1 hour (or longer, depending on marinating)
Serves 8

1 Place the fish and raisins in a large bowl, add 2 tablespoons olive oil and the orange zest and juice, and season well. Carefully toss the fish to coat, cover, and leave to marinate for 30 minutes or up to 2 hours. Preheat the oven to 200°C/180°C fan/gas 6.
2 Meanwhile, place the peppers in a large, shallow roasting tin and drizzle with the remaining olive oil. Season, toss together and roast in the oven for 30 minutes.
3 Arrange the fish and raisins on top of the peppers and pour over the juices. Scatter the pine nuts over and season with a good pinch of salt. Cook in the oven for 12–15 minutes until the fish is just cooked through. Scatter with parsley and bring to the table.

• Per serving 407 kcalories, protein 41g, carbohydrate 15g, fat 21g, saturated fat 3g, fibre 2g, added sugar none, salt 0.3g

Fresh tomatoes and garlic cook down to sweet, saucy pan juices in this sophisticated but so easy recipe.

Italian chicken with ham, basil and beans

8 skinless chicken thighs, bone in
1 large bunch of fresh basil
8 slices prosciutto or other
dry-cured ham
2 tbsp olive oil
2 garlic bulbs, halved across
the middle
800g/1lb 12oz mix yellow and
red tomatoes, halved or
quartered if large
175ml/6fl oz dry white wine
400g can cannellini or other white
beans, drained and rinsed

Takes about 1½ hours • Serves 4

1 Season the chicken thighs. Pinch off eight basil sprigs and lay one on top of each chicken thigh. Wrap each thigh in a piece of ham, with the ends tucked underneath.
2 Preheat the oven to 160°C/140°C fan/gas 3. Heat the oil over a medium heat in a large roasting tin. Add the chicken and fry for 4 minutes each side or until the ham is just crisped and the chicken lightly golden.
3 Add the tomatoes, garlic, half the remaining basil leaves and the wine. Season, cover with foil, then cook in the oven for 40 minutes.
4 Take out of the oven; turn the temperature up to 220°C/200°C fan/gas 7. Remove the foil then stir the beans into the tomatoey juices. Return to the oven, uncovered, and cook for 30 minutes until the tomatoes, chicken and garlic are starting to crisp and chicken is very tender. Scatter over the remaining basil.

• Per serving 455 kcalories, protein 55g, carbohydrate 22g, fat 16g, saturated fat 4g, fibre 6g, sugar 10g, salt 1.79g

Once you're prepped, this dish only takes about 10 minutes to cook, so it's perfect for casual last-minute entertaining. Serve with a salad, if you like.

Chunky chilli wraps

1 tbsp vegetable oil, plus a few extra drizzles
750g/1lb 10oz rump steak, sliced into thin strips
1 red onion, roughly chopped
4 mild green chillies, seeded and chopped
1 tsp cumin seeds
1 tsp cayenne or hot chilli powder
400g can chopped tomatoes
420g can red kidney beans, drained and rinsed
200g/8oz roasted peppers from a jar, cut into strips
1 tsp Worcestershire sauce

TO SERVE
12 flour tortillas, warmed
284ml pot soured cream
a handful of fresh mint, roughly chopped

Takes 35–45 minutes • Serves 6

1 Heat the oil in a wok until hot. Tip in a third of the beef and stir-fry for 2–3 minutes until it begins to brown. Scoop out the beef and put it on a plate. Repeat with the remaining beef, adding a drizzle more oil to the pan each time.
2 Toss the onion, chillies, cumin seeds and cayenne or chilli powder into the pan, stir and sizzle for 2 minutes. Lower the heat, tip in the tomatoes, kidney beans and roasted peppers. Return the beef to the pan and cook for 2 minutes, stirring occasionally, until bubbling. Add the Worcestershire sauce and continue to simmer gently for a further 2 minutes. Season to taste.
3 To serve, heat the tortillas according to the packet instructions. Pass round the warm tortillas for wrapping up the chilli, and bowls of soured cream and mint for drizzling and scattering over.

• Per serving 644 kcalories, protein 38g, carbohydrate 54g, fat 32g, saturated fat 13g, fibre 6g, added sugar none, salt 2.89g

You'll often see lamb shanks on restaurant menus; this is because they're great value and will transform into a fantastic meal with very little effort. Make them the day before for a really full flavour.

Red wine braised lamb shanks

2 tbsp olive oil
4 lamb shanks
2 large onions, sliced
1 carrot, peeled and sliced
1 celery stick, sliced
2 garlic cloves, sliced
250ml/9fl oz full-bodied red wine
250ml/9fl oz beef or lamb stock
175ml/6fl oz tomato passata
1 tsp golden caster sugar
1 bay leaf
1 fresh thyme sprig
chopped flatleaf parsley, to garnish

Takes 2½ hours • Serves 4

1 Preheat the oven to 160°C/140°C fan/gas 3. Put a large casserole dish over a high heat with 1 tablespoon olive oil. Add the lamb shanks and brown really well on all sides. Remove and set aside.

2 Reduce the heat, add the remaining olive oil and the sliced onions, carrot and celery. Cook for 5 minutes until the vegetables are mostly tender. Add the garlic and continue to cook for a further minute.

3 Pour the red wine into the pan, boil, then simmer for 3 minutes. Add the stock, passata, sugar, bay leaf, thyme and seasoning, and bring back to the boil. Add the lamb shanks, coating them in the braising liquid. Cover with a tight-fitting lid and braise for about 2 hours or until the meat is really tender, turning the meat in the liquid every 30 minutes. Check the seasoning, scatter with parsley and serve.

• Per serving 460 kcalories, protein 37g, carbohydrate 15g, fat 24g, saturated fat 10g, fibre 3g, added sugar 2g, salt 1g

Try this for a stress-free lunch that's sure to impress.

Warm duck salad with walnut and orange dressing

4 duck breasts
4 medium potatoes, peeled and diced
16 walnut halves
250g pack vacuum-packed cooked beetroot (without vinegar), cut into wedges
100g bag watercress, large stems removed
4 spring onions, thinly sliced
1 chicory head, separated into leaves and the core sliced
3 small oranges, peeled and sliced

FOR THE DRESSING
4 tbsp walnut oil
4 tsp red wine vinegar
1 tbsp chunky marmalade

Takes 35 minutes • Serves 4

1 Mix together all the dressing ingredients, season, then set aside.
2 Heat a roasting pan on the hob, add the duck, skin-side down, then gently fry for around 10 minutes. Turn the duck over for a second to seal, then remove.
3 Preheat the oven to 220°C/200°C fan/gas 7. Toss the potatoes in the duck fat and fry until golden. Lift out of the fat with a slotted spoon and discard the fat. Put the potatoes, nuts and beetroot back into the pan. Put the duck on a roasting rack above the veg. Roast for 15 minutes.
4 Toss together the watercress, spring onions, chicory and oranges with most of the dressing. Pile on to plates with the beetroot, potatoes and walnuts. Slice the duck, arrange on top of the salad and drizzle with the remaining dressing. Serve warm.

• Per serving 742 kcalories, protein 34g, carbohydrate 40g, fat 51g, saturated fat 10g, fibre 6g, sugar 18g, salt 0.54g

If you know you want to serve a warming stew but fancy trying something different, this dish is for you. Just serve it with a big bowl of rice and let your guests help themselves.

Chinese-style braised beef

3 pak choi heads, halved
3–4 tbsp olive oil
6 garlic cloves, thinly sliced
a good thumb-sized knob of ginger, peeled and shredded
1 bunch spring onions, sliced
1 red chilli, seeded and thinly sliced
1.5kg/3lb 5oz braising beef, well marbled and cut into large pieces
2 tbsp plain flour, well seasoned
1 tsp Chinese five spice powder
2 star anise
2 tsp light muscovado sugar (or use whatever you've got)
3 tbsp Chinese cooking wine or dry sherry
3 tbsp dark soy sauce, plus more to taste
500ml/18fl oz beef stock

Takes about 2½ hours • Serves 6

1 Bring 2cm water to boil in a large casserole, then simmer the pak choi for 4 minutes. Drain, cool under cold water; set aside.

2 Heat 2 tablespoons oil in the pan. Fry the garlic, ginger, onions and chilli for 3 minutes then set aside. Toss the beef with flour, add more oil to the pan, then brown in batches, about 5 minutes each time, and set aside.

3 Add the spices, fry for 1 minute, then tip in the gingery mix. Tip in the sugar and beef, then stir. Splash in the wine or sherry. Preheat the oven to 150°C/130°C fan/gas 2.

4 Pour in the soy sauce and stock and boil. Tightly cover the pan then braise in the oven for 1½–2 hours, stirring halfway, until meltingly soft. Nestle the pak choi into the sauce, then leave for a few minutes, lid on, to warm through. Season with extra soy sauce before serving.

• Per serving 513 kcalories, protein 54g, carbohydrate 9g, fat 29g, saturated fat 10g, fibre 1g, sugar 4g, salt 2.39g

Leeks are at their loveliest when slow cooked – they virtually melt into this stunning pot roast, perfect for friends to share.

All-in-one leek and pork pot roast

1kg/2lb 4oz boned and rolled shoulder joint of pork
6 bay leaves
2 garlic cloves, sliced
1 bunch of fresh thyme sprigs
25g/1oz butter
sunflower oil
2 onions, peeled and cut into wedges
5 juniper berries, crushed
1 tsp golden caster sugar
1 tbsp white wine vinegar
4 whole leeks, trimmed then each cut into 3
250ml/9fl oz white wine

Takes 2¼ hours • Serves 6

1 Preheat the oven to 180°C/160°C fan/gas 4. Untie and unroll the joint then lay four bay leaves, the sliced garlic and half the thyme sprigs along the centre of the meat. Retie with string.
2 Heat the butter and 1 tablespoon oil in a casserole, then brown the pork on all sides; about 10 minutes. Add the onions, then cook for 5 minutes. Add the juniper berries, sugar and vinegar. Simmer, then tuck the leeks, remaining bay and thyme around the pork. Add the wine, cover, then cook in the oven for 1½–1¾ hours until the meat is tender.
3 To serve, remove the meat to a board. Season the veg, then use a slotted spoon to lift it into a bowl. Serve generous slices of meat with the bowl of vegetables and the sauce on the side.

• Per serving 470 kcalories, protein 32g, carbohydrate 9g, fat 33g, saturated fat 13g, fibre 3g, sugar 7g, salt 0.36g

Swap the usual spuds and gravy for warmly spiced veg and tasty nuggets of chorizo in this aromatic autumnal roast.

Roast chicken with butternut squash, chorizo and chilli

4 medium red onions, 1 halved, the rest cut into wedges
12 fresh sage leaves, 8 shredded, 4 left whole, plus more to garnish
1 large whole chicken, about 2.25kg/5lb
1 tbsp olive oil, plus extra for greasing
1 butternut squash, peeled and cut into large chunky wedges
500g pack Charlotte potatoes, halved
2 red chillies, seeds left in and sliced
110g pack chorizo sausage, sliced
1 garlic bulb, separated into cloves

Takes 2½ hours • Serves 6

1 Preheat the oven to 190°C/170°C fan/gas 5. Tuck two onion halves and four sage leaves inside the chicken cavity, rub the skin with a little oil, then season. Cook in the oven in a large roasting tin, breast-side down for 45 minutes. Turn over then roast for around 30 minutes more.
2 Toss the onion wedges with the shredded sage, squash, potatoes, chillies, chorizo, garlic cloves, 1 tablespoon oil and seasoning. Scatter round the chicken, toss in the pan juices; roast for 45 minutes.
3 Set the chicken aside to rest, turn the oven up to 220°C/200°C fan/gas 7. Toss the vegetables in the pan juices, spread over the tin to give them a bit of space, then return to the oven for 15 minutes to brown. Garnish the chicken with fresh sage leaves and serve.

• Per serving 501 kcalories, protein 42g, carbohydrate 30g, fat 25g, saturated fat 8g, fibre 4g, sugar 11g, salt 0.57g

This is so easy to prepare and the dish almost looks after itself – the end result is packed with flavour.

Herby baked lamb in tomato sauce

1.8kg/4lb–2kg/4lb 8oz shoulder
of lamb
2 tbsp olive oil
3 fresh oregano sprigs, leaves
stripped from 2
3 fresh rosemary sprigs, leaves
stripped from 2
3 garlic cloves, roughly chopped
600ml/1 pint red wine
2 × 400g cans chopped tomatoes
1 tbsp caster sugar

Takes 4¼ hours • Serves 4
(with leftovers)

1 Preheat the oven to 220°C/200°C fan/ gas 7. Put the lamb into a large ovenproof dish. Whiz the oil, oregano, rosemary leaves, garlic and seasoning in a food processor. Rub all over the lamb; roast for 20 minutes. Cover, lower the oven to 150°C/130°C fan/ gas 2, then roast for 3 hours more.
2 Remove from the oven, spoon off the fat, leaving any meat juices in the pan. Add the wine, tomatoes and remaining herb sprigs, then return to the oven, uncovered, for 40 minutes more. The lamb should now be meltingly tender. Carefully transfer the lamb to a plate; cover and leave to rest.
3 Meanwhile, simmer the sauce for around 10–15 minutes until thickened. Season with the sugar, and a little salt and pepper, then return the lamb to the pan to serve.

• Per serving 595 kcalories, protein 42g, carbohydrate 11g, fat 40g, saturated fat 19g, fibre 1g, sugar 10g, salt 0.51g

This simple recipe is ideal for a special midweek supper, as it can be cooked very quickly when you get home from work. Any leftover sauce is stunning saved and used on pizzas or folded through pasta.

Sirloin steaks with pizzaiola sauce

50ml/2fl oz olive oil
1 garlic clove, roughly chopped
4 sirloin steaks, each about 140g/5oz
2 × 400g cans chopped tomatoes
2 tsp dried oregano
bread or new potatoes, to serve
rocket leaves, to garnish

Takes 30 minutes • Serves 4

1 Heat a heavy-based frying pan over a high heat, then add the olive oil and garlic. Season the meat and then, two at a time, quickly brown the steaks in the pan on both sides.
2 Put all four steaks in the pan, add the tomatoes, season with salt and pepper, then turn down the heat. Sprinkle the oregano over the meat and tomatoes, partially cover the pan, then simmer gently for 10 minutes.
3 Lift the tender pieces of meat from the pan, cover with foil, then set aside. Increase the heat, then simmer the tomato sauce for about 10 minutes, until it has reduced by half. Spoon the sauce over the steak and serve with bread or new potatoes and a garnish of rocket leaves.

• Per serving 415 kcalories, protein 33g, carbohydrate 5g, fat 29g, saturated fat 10g, fibre 2g, sugar 4g, salt 0.63g

Our big beef casserole is all the beefier for its crisp Marmite toasts. Like any stew, it's even better left to cool and then chilled overnight, which also spreads the workload.

Marmite carbonade

85g/3oz unsalted butter, plus extra for spreading
4 onions, halved and sliced
3 garlic cloves, peeled and smashed
1.5kg/3lb 5oz stewing steak, cut into large cubes
850ml/1½ pints beef stock
1½ tbsp plain flour
400ml can stout
about 10 fresh thyme sprigs, tied into a bunch
2 bay leaves
1 tbsp light muscovado sugar
2 tsp red wine vinegar
2–4 tbsp mushroom ketchup
1 celery heart, trimmed and sliced
about 2 tsp Marmite
about ¾ baguette, cut into 25 or so thin slices

Takes 2 hours 50 minutes • Serves 8

1 Preheat the oven to 180°C/160°C fan/gas 4. Melt half the butter in a casserole. Gently fry the onions for 8–12 minutes; add the garlic for 1 minute then tip into a bowl. Increase the heat, and brown the beef in batches, adding butter each time. Deglaze the pan as you go: splash a little stock into the pan, stir, then tip into a bowl.
2 Return the onions and beef to the pan, stir in the flour, then pour over stout, stock and deglazing liquid. Add the herbs, sugar, vinegar and mushroom ketchup. Season, bring to the boil, cover, then cook in the oven for 1½ hours. Skim off any fat.
3 Turn the oven up to 200°C/180°C fan/gas 6. Discard the herbs, then add the celery. Mix the remaining butter with the Marmite, then spread over the bread. Place on top of the stew and cook for 30–40 minutes.

• Per serving 520 kcalories, protein 44g, carbohydrate 24g, fat 27g, saturated fat 13g, fibre 2g, sugar 7g, salt 1.3g

Don't be daunted by cooking whole fish – this special main course
is easy to make and sure to impress.

Whole roast bream with potatoes and olives

400g/14oz new or small potatoes,
thickly sliced
2 tbsp olive oil
a large handful of pitted small
black olives
1 garlic clove, chopped
1 large bunch of flatleaf parsley,
leaves roughly chopped,
stalks reserved
zest of ½ lemon
1 whole sea bream, about 450g/1lb,
gutted, head on (ask your
fishmonger to do this for you)
1 small glass of white wine

Takes 50 minutes • Serves 2
(easily doubled)

1 Preheat the oven to 220°C/200°C fan/
gas 7. Put the potatoes in a gratin dish,
toss with 1 tablespoon oil then roast for
20 minutes until just starting to soften. Toss
the olives, garlic, half the chopped parsley,
the lemon zest and some salt and pepper
with the potatoes then spread over the dish.
2 Season the fish and place the parsley
stalks in the cavity. Lay the fish on top of the
potatoes and drizzle with the rest of the olive
oil. Bake for 15 minutes. Pour the wine over,
then return to the oven for 10 minutes more
until the potatoes have browned and the fish
is cooked.
3 Remove the dish from the oven, scatter
over the rest of the parsley and bring the dish
to the table. When you serve up, don't forget
the lovely white wine juices in the bottom of
the dish.

• Per serving 463 kcalories, protein 34g, carbohydrate 36g,
fat 20g, saturated fat 3g, fibre 3g, sugar 6g, salt 0.81g

If you want to cook this irresistibly easy lamb for four, simply double the ingredients and make sure you use a large-enough pan.

Feta-crusted lamb with rich tomato sauce

7- or 8-bone rack of lamb, trimmed of fat, then cut into two racks
2 tbsp extra-virgin olive oil, plus extra to drizzle
a few fresh thyme sprigs, left whole, plus extra to serve
4 garlic cloves, crushed
zest of 1 lemon
1 tsp dried oregano, plus a pinch
20g pack flat-leaf parsley, stalks finely chopped, leaves roughly
400g can cherry tomatoes
50g/2oz feta, finely crumbled
½ slice white bread (day old if you can), whizzed into crumbs

Takes 50 minutes, plus marinating and resting • Serves 2

1 Put the racks into a food bag along with 1 tablespoon oil, the thyme sprigs, half the garlic, zest and oregano. Chill for 30 minutes or up to 24 hours. Make sure the lamb has returned to room temperature before cooking.
2 Heat a casserole dish; add 1 tablespoon oil. Add the remaining garlic and the parsley stalks; soften for 1 minute. Add the tomatoes and pinch of oregano; simmer for 5 minutes. Add half the parsley leaves. Heat the oven to 230°C/210°C fan/gas 8. Meanwhile, mix the remaining parsley, zest and oregano, plus the feta and crumbs to make a crust.
3 Season the meat, then press the crust on. Sit the racks in the sauce, crust-side up. Strew the extra thyme sprigs over, then drizzle with oil. Roast uncovered for 20 minutes until golden and the sauce thickened. Rest for 10 minutes, then serve.

• Per serving 582 kcalories, protein 26g, carbohydrate 12g, fat 48g, saturated fat 18g, fibre 3g, sugar 6g, salt 1.47g

Guinea fowl is widely available, but you could easily use a
medium-sized chicken in this autumnal one-pot instead.

Guinea fowl with roast chestnuts

1 guinea fowl or chicken,
about 1.3kg/3lb
½ large lemon
2 bay leaves
several fresh thyme sprigs
3 tbsp olive oil
500g/1lb 2oz potatoes, unpeeled, cut
into chunks
3 garlic cloves, unpeeled and bruised
200g/8oz chestnut mushrooms,
halved if large
200g/8oz vacuum-packed cooked
chestnuts

FOR THE SAUCE
150ml/¼ pint white wine
150ml/¼ pint chicken stock
1 tbsp bramble or redcurrant jelly

Takes 2 hours • Serves 4

1 Preheat the oven to 190°C/170°C fan/
gas 5. Season the meat, put the lemon half,
the bay leaves and two sprigs of thyme inside
the bird. Set in a roasting tin, drizzle with a
little olive oil, then roast for 15 minutes.
2 Meanwhile, strip the remaining thyme
leaves from their stalks. Mix together the
potatoes, thyme, garlic and remaining oil,
then season. Put the potatoes around the
bird, then roast for 45 minutes more.
3 Stir the mushrooms into the potatoes
along with the chestnuts. Roast for a further
15 minutes until the mushrooms are cooked.
Lift the bird and veg out of the pan on to a
serving platter and keep warm.
4 Boil the pan juices on the hob, add the wine,
stock and jelly, then bring to the boil, stirring
to dissolve the jelly. Boil hard until the sauce is
slightly thickened. Season to taste, then serve.

• Per serving 633 kcalories, protein 56g, carbohydrate 45g,
fat 24g, saturated fat 6g, fibre 5g, sugar 9g, salt 0.56g

Give ice cream an Italian twist with this easy coffee-flavoured chocolatey dessert. It's so good you might want to make double!

Broken biscotti ice cream with hot mocha

500ml tub good-quality vanilla ice cream
12 biscotti biscuits
100g bar good-quality dark chocolate
2 tbsp brandy
200ml/7fl oz (about 1 mug) freshly made strong coffee

Takes 10 minutes • Serves 4

1 Leave the ice cream out of the freezer for 5 minutes to soften, then tip into a bowl. Put six of the biscuits into a freezer bag, squeeze out the air, then bash the biscuits into crumbs. Fold into the ice cream then return to the freezer.
2 Break the chocolate into a pan, add the brandy and heat gently until melted. Stir (it will thicken), then pour in the hot coffee and carry on stirring until it becomes a smooth mocha.
3 Scoop the ice cream into heatproof glasses or bowls, then pour the mocha over. Serve straight away with the remaining biscotti on the side.

• Per serving 349 kcalories, protein 6g, carbohydrate 38g, fat 19g, saturated fat 11g, fibre 2g, sugar 26g, salt 0.26g

Gently infused spice transforms the humble pear into a wonderful winter dessert. Serve with scoops of ice cream or a drizzle of cream.

Star anise and lemon pears

zest and juice of 1 lemon
140g/5oz golden caster sugar
4 star anise
4 ripe pears

Takes 1 hour • Serves 4

1 Thinly peel the zest from the lemon with a potato peeler and put the zest in a pan with the sugar, star anise and 1 litre (1¾ pints) water. Bring to the boil, then leave to infuse for 5 minutes.

2 Peel and core the pears, leaving the stem on, then lower into the syrup. Cover and leave to cook on a gentle heat for 10 minutes or until the pears are tender. Lift the pears from the pan, then boil the liquid over a high heat until syrupy. Squeeze the juice from the lemon into the syrup, then pour over the pears. Eat warm or chilled.

• Per serving 205 kcalories, protein 1g, carbohydrate 53g, fat none, saturated fat none, fibre 3g, added sugar 37g, salt 0.02g

This is the ultimate cheat's dessert; it tastes every bit as gorgeous as a full-blown fruit pie, without all the work and washing up.

Rhubarb, ginger and apple scrunch pie

butter, for greasing
375g pack ready-rolled shortcrust pastry
400g/14oz Bramley apples, sliced
400g pack trimmed rhubarb, cut into lengths
100g/4oz demerara sugar, plus extra for sprinkling
2 balls stem ginger, chopped
2 tbsp cornflour
milk, for brushing
custard, to serve

Takes 1 hour • Serves 6

1 Preheat the oven to 180°C/160°C fan/gas 4 and grease a large baking sheet. Unroll the pastry and place it flat on the baking sheet.
2 Mix the apple slices and the rhubarb with the sugar, ginger and cornflour, then pile into the centre of the pastry. Gather up the sides of the pastry to enclose the fruit so that the pie looks like a rough tart (you need to work with the size and shape of the pastry, so it will be more of an oblong shape than round).
3 Brush the pastry with milk and scatter with demerara. Bake for 35 minutes until the pastry is golden and the fruit is tender. Cut into slices and serve with custard.

• Per serving 397 kcalories, protein 4g, carbohydrate 59g, fat 18g, saturated fat 9g, fibre 4g, added sugar 18g, salt 0.27g

A fabulous dinner-party pudding all year round. Use a pack of frozen summer berries if you're cooking this outside of the soft-fruit season; just let them thaw at room temperature for 20 minutes first.

Iced berries with white chocolate sauce

350g/12oz mixed summer berries
100g/4oz white chocolate, broken
into pieces
2 tbsp double cream

Takes 25 minutes • Serves 4

1 Pile the berries into pretty glasses or on to plates and freeze for 20 minutes. The berries should become iced but not frozen solid.
2 When ready to serve, put the chocolate in a non-metallic bowl with the cream and microwave on High for 1 minute. Check to see if it is soft enough to stir into a sauce, if not, give it 30 seconds then stir again. Add more cream, if you like. Leave to cool slightly, stirring occasionally. To serve, pour the chocolate sauce over the iced berries.

• Per serving 194 kcalories, protein 3g, carbohydrate 20g, fat 12g, saturated fat 7g, fibre 2g, added sugar 12g, salt 0.08g

Any selection of fruit works with this dip. Try berries in the summer or marshmallows and bite-sized pieces of cake in colder months.

Dark chocolate fondue with crushed nuts and tropical fruits

200g/8oz plain chocolate
50g/2oz butter
2 tbsp Malibu or white rum
½ mango, peeled and cubed
½ papaya, peeled and cubed
8 physalis (also known as Cape gooseberries)
200g pack pineapple chunks (or cut your own fresh pineapple)
50g/2oz toasted crushed hazelnuts

Takes 15 minutes • Serves 4

1 Put the chocolate, butter, alcohol and 75ml/2½fl oz water into a heatproof bowl set above a pan of gently simmering water. Make sure the bottom of the bowl doesn't touch the water. Let it sit for 5–10 minutes, stirring occasionally until smooth.
2 Arrange the fruit on a platter with a bowl of the crushed nuts and forks or cocktail sticks ready for dipping. Dip the fruit chunks into the chocolate and then the nuts, and pop them straight into your mouth (or someone else's!).

• Per serving 505 kcalories, protein 5g, carbohydrate 47g, fat 32g, saturated fat 15g, fibre 4g, sugar 46g, salt 0.21g

Index

Picture and recipe credits